BORDER DIALOGUES

Born and educated in Britain, Iain Chambers now lives and teaches in Italy. Italy, he says, has allowed him to look back on Britain with different eyes, opening up an intellectual itinerary through a decade of crisis – of Marxism, of reason, of modernism. Writing from two shores and between two cultures, he proposes a journey into some of the territories of contemporary culture, philosophy and criticism.

The essays in *Border Dialogues* lead to encounters with Nietzsche and Italian 'weak thought', with the mysteries of being 'British', and with more immediate concerns such as computers, fashion, gender, and ethnicity. Squarely based within the debate on modernism and postmodernism, the writings also open questions on contemporary culture and politics within an ethical and ecological framework. Iain Chambers explores how such different strands come together in an increasingly shared network, and how this mix can lead to an interrogation and rethinking of contemporary critical sense.

This innovative reading of postmodernity offers a dialogue with voices largely unknown in Anglo-American circles, and will be of particular interest to students of critical theory, cultural studies, radical philosophy, and deconstruction.

Iain Chambers teaches courses on contemporary British culture, cultural theory, and æsthetics at the Istituto Universitario Orientale in Naples, Italy. He is author of *Urban Rhythms: Pop Music and Popular Culture* (1985) and *Popular Culture: The Metropolitan Experience* (1986).

Comedia
Series editor: David Morley

Border Dialogues

Journeys in postmodernity

Iain Chambers

A Comedia book
published by Routledge
London and New York

A Comedia book
First published in 1990
by Routledge
11 New Fetter Lane, London EC4P 4EE

Simultaneously published in the USA and Canada
by Routledge
a division of Routledge, Chapman and Hall, Inc.
29 West 35th Street, New York, NY 10001

© 1990 Iain Chambers

Typeset in 10/12pt Palatino by Columns of Reading
Printed in Great Britain by
Richard Clay Ltd, Bungay, Suffolk

British Library Cataloguing in Publication Data
Chambers, Iain
Border dialogues: journeys in postmodernity. – (A comedia
book)
1. Culture. Postmodernism
I. Title
306
ISBN 0–415–03554–6
ISBN 0–415–01375–5 (pbk)

Library of Congress Cataloging in Publication Data
Chambers, Iain.
Border dialogues: journeys in postmodernity / by Iain Chambers.
p. cm.
"A Comedia book."
Includes bibliographical references.
ISBN 0–415–03554–6. —ISBN 0–415–01375–5 (pbk.)
1. Postmodernism. 2. Philosophy, Modern – 20th century.
3. Civilization, Modern – 1950– I. Title.
B831.2.C42 1990
190'.9'04—dc20   89–70137

Contents

Acknowledgements

I wish to thank Catherine Hall, Meaghan Morris, Marina Vitale, Larry Grossberg, Dick Hebdige, Nelson Moe and Paolo Prato for their comments, criticisms and suggestions; my editor Dave Morley for putting up with my uncertainties and constant changing of mind; students at the Istituto Universitario Orientale, Naples, for accepting some of the things that I said and transforming them into stimulating possibilities; and Lidia Curti for all this and much more besides.

I would also like to thank the editors of *Anglistica, Block, Cultural Studies, il Manifesto, New Formations* and Larry Grossberg at Champaign for initially giving me the opportunity to develop some of the arguments in this book.

The translations from Italian are mine.

I think it was Rilke who so lamented the inadequacy of our symbolism – regretted so bitterly we cannot, unlike the (was it?) Ancient Greeks, find adequate external symbols for the life within us – yes, that's the quotation. But, no. He was wrong. Our external symbols must always express the life within us with absolute precision; how could they do otherwise, since that life has generated them? Therefore we must not blame our poor symbols if they take forms that seem trivial to us, or absurd, for the symbols themselves have no control over their own fleshy manifestations, however paltry they may be; the nature of our life alone has determined their forms.

A critique of these symbols is a critique of our lives.

Angela Carter, *The Passion of New Eve*

Philosophers have sought to express with the concept of act (or of the incarnation that makes it possible) this descent into the real, which the concept of thought interpreted as a pure knowing would maintain only as a play of lights. The act of thought – thought as an act – would precede the thought thinking or becoming conscious of an act. The notion of act involves a violence essentially: the violence of transitivity, lacking in the transcendence of thought. For the transcendence of thought remains closed in itself despite all its adventures – which in the last analysis are purely imaginary, or are adventures traversed as by Ulysses: on the way home. What, in action, breaks forth as essential violence is the surplus of being over the thought that claims to contain it, the marvel of the idea of infinity.

Emmanuel Lévinas, *Totality and Infinity*

Years ago
I was an angry young man
And I'd pretend
That I was a billboard
Standing tall
By the side of the road
And I fell in love
With a beautiful highway.

Talking Heads, *(Nothing But) Flowers*

Chapter 1

The 'double solution'

In Derek Jarman's film *Caravaggio* (1986), the text – Caravaggio's paintings, his biography – dissolves into an extensive textuality. The film itself, its lighting and *chiaroscuro* effects, become an example of the Caravaggio-esque. As a young painter, Caravaggio is initially presented as an early seventeenth-century, homosexual, 'wild boy', simultaneously a street punk (on his knife is inscribed the motto, 'No hope, no fear') and a self-proclaimed 'work of art'. This is supplemented by type-writers, train whistles, cigarettes and a paper hat made from an old copy of *L'Unità*. These are all found in a Rome of the early 1600s: anachronisms that constitute a recognizable 'Italianicity'. (All the sounds, including that of the rain, were recorded in Italy, while the film was shot in a warehouse on the Isle of Dogs.) Such signs blatantly refuse the rules of the pedantic antiquarian. The feel of the film is itself distinctly baroque. In its decentring of perspective and sense of excess the film proposes a disturbing affinity with both the birth of that epoch and the climate of the late twentieth century. This is hardly parody or pastiche but rather an intelligent seizure of the traces of the past that flare up in the present. For the film proposes a representation of a Caravaggio that is comprehensible, hence complex and fragmentary and not the solid referent of a traditional art discourse, a Hollywood film or a neat historical tale.

This example of the apparently disordered detail and vertiginous experience of the baroque is also a sign of our times. Today, as then, we are witnesses to the ruins of previous orders of meaning that come to be re-elaborated, extended and ultimately undone. We are left turning over the traces, unwilling to succumb to their fading authority yet at the same time unsure of what lies in their abandon. The hard die of the rationalism we have inherited, once presented as the unique, progressive and symmetrical appropriation of reality, has been softened up, submerged and thwarted in an excess of sense, in a short-circuiting and confusion of connections. One of the more recent symptoms of this breakup, and breaking-out, has been the recourse to the fictional, æsthetic and literary modes in recent critical writing. The languages of criticism are no longer understood to be transparent. They, too, are overloaded and uncertain about what is it they are representing. They, like the reality they seek to reveal, have turned in upon themselves, become suspect, even neurotic, seeking to conspire with the complexity they sense.

There are numerous strands involved in this move away from taking language and discourse for granted, as though they provide an unproblematic access to reality. Such a problematization of reality is certainly not, despite the attention it has recently received in the debate over postmodernism, a recent development. There are clamorous precedents in philosophy that, on the one hand, develop out of Nietzsche's critique of analytical enquiry and its metaphysics, and, on the other, out of Wittgenstein's reflections on the limits of language; there is the ideological critique developed in Marxism; and there is the foundation of psychoanalysis based on another, repressed, language, that of the unconscious. In all these particular interrogations, 'reality' is not so readily available.

To this history we need to add the presence and persistent interrogation of the 'other', the unknown and the unanswered, the inscrutable and indecipherable, which in modern European thought has invariably, together with race, been represented by the 'feminine'. As a metaphor of disruption and transgression the latter usually 'bears no direct or even necessary relation to real-life women'.[1] Still, it is has largely been the encounter between the transgression of post-Nietzschean thought and, often unacknowledged, 'real-life' encounters with the repressed histories, languages and voices represented by women, ethnicity (the 'Jew', the 'Black'), and the non-Western world in general, that increasingly form the secret challenge to critical discourse.

What the alternatives to the traditional language of criticism and thought share is a common focus on what Friedrich Nietzsche referred to as the 'school of suspect' and its intention of removing the mask from immediate appearances. Of course, subsequent debate lies precisely in what it is that we find behind the mask. For classical Marxism it is the 'real' relations of the social world governed by the regulatory mechanisms of a particular mode of production. Central to this particular idea of unveiling the 'real' is the theme of authenticity. The Marxist critique that penetrates the mask lays the basis for a social alternative to emerge in which men and women would come to fully reappropriate themselves in a world stripped of false appearances and the fetishizing rule of commodities. This suggests, although now in a materialist language, the Hegelian belief that truth lies in a total synthesis; in this case, the ideological critique seeks to recompose a non-alienated totality in order to arrive at a complete or non-partial point of view. As Gianni Vattimo, critic of such totalizing aspirations, and proponent of a 'weaker' mode of reasoning, points out, ideology here is not only considered to be false because it hides the truth, but also because it involves *partial* and incomplete thought.[2]

With psychoanalysis there is a more complex enquiry that takes us behind the self-referring individual of modern rationalism to an unstable knowledge encountered in the dreams, drives and desires of our secret, psychic life. The fundamental problem for both Freudian analysis and the Marxist critique of reality, is that when examining the distinction between symptoms and sources, between the symbol and what is symbolized, where can we say that appearances stop? Jacques Derrida has convincingly argued that what is presented as a logical or scientific 'truth' is itself a rhetorical device, an effect of language that seeks to negate its status as language precisely in order to better its claim on the real.[3]

The author of the *Interpretation of Dreams* depended, for example, on the stories his patients told him; he analysed not a dream but a recollection, a fragmented narrative, a fiction. Freud himself acknowledged this deep-seated ambiguity in his analytical writings, underlining the infinite and whirling play of language that carries with it the strange sensation of losing oneself as sense is transformed, rewritten, and proliferates in interpretation. When Freud speaks of the dream, he is referring not to the actual dream itself, but to its reconstruction, to the elements that constitute the space of memory in the present. What is important is not so much what happened – in the dream, in childhood – as the particular account or the narrative that the patient presents to the analyst. It is that material which is interpreted; 'reality', what actually might have happened, is no longer immediately available. It has been rewritten and displaced by a construction that comes to be represented in the second order of a discourse that simultaneously claims theoretical status and yet so often reads like a novel.[4]

This, against the naturalist and regulatory assumptions of the later institution of psychoanalysis, proposes a critical language in which the poetics of the symbol becomes central. In what Freud defines as *Verleugnung* the symbol constitutes a refusal, a repudiation or negation, of the real. For what the symbol offers is the infinite language of the double, the uncanny, the disguised, the displaced. Here the symbol is not the medium of communication but is rather something that disturbs communication. The symbol's relationship with the principles of communication is encompassed in an endless game of 'montage and sabotage': 'In the repudiation the disguised displacement winks at the reality principle.'[5]

The further and more notorious response that emerges from the 'school of suspect' is that behind the mask there is nothing; that there is in fact no elsewhere in which we can locate the 'truth'. This stark vision is summed up in the Nietzschean proclamation that 'God is dead'. In this 'critique of the critique' (Nietzsche) there is no longer a transcendental structure, a priori synthesis or metaphysical guarantee to protect us from ourselves and the world *we* have made. There exists no reality beyond appearances. In this extreme secularization of analytical languages, where a metaphysical violence imposed in the name of a transcendental 'reality' or the 'Truth' is refused, it is language itself, our constructions, narratives, the stories we tell each other, that tends towards becoming what Derrida terms the factor of truth. Here we are talking about a sense of reality which is not something that can be reduced to the formal dialectic of reason, history, progress, and the 'authentic' or 'original' foundations of abstract being, but is rather something that becomes, that emerges through difference, through specificity, through dialogue, through our languages and histories; that is, in the insistent intercourse of the world.

This sense of dialogue and the becoming of 'truth' was once suggestively set out in an alternative version of the Œdipus myth offered by Friedrich Hölderlin. The tragedy of Œdipus, according to the German poet, lies not in the fact of patricide or incest, but in his persistent interrogation of the blind prophet Tiresias. In his insistence on arriving at the bottom of things Œdipus condemns himself to be the victim of the same abstract law that drives him to violently extract the truth at all costs. Œdipus's indiscretion before the oracle of Thebes leads him to find the 'double solution which establishes once and for all our final ambivalence': first, before the Sphinx, there is the solution that permits him to avoid death; then there is the solution, torn from the seer, that condemns him to death. Œdipus's questioning presents us with a world full of infinite interpretations. But in this world he seeks a final answer, he is set on 'the demented research for knowledge'.[6] It is not by chance that Œdipus becomes one of the primordial emblems of the Occident.

> Only Œdipus can avoid death by the oracle, only Œdipus is able to be condemned to death by the oracle. The inseparable link between the two solutions supports the entire idea of the resolutory capacity of thought, it is a situation in which we still find ourselves today.[7]

Alongside the Freudian account and the founding myth of modern psychoanalysis the phallus here returns in the thirst for complete knowledge, in the blind obedience to the authority of logos and its hegemony of vision.

The origin of the essays in this book lies somewhere in here, in this world of the 'double solution' in which there is no obvious or metaphysical 'truth', no absolute or pure sense to guide and orientate us; where, in the encounter with possible meanings, diverse, asymmetrical signs and histories propose a constant sense of difference, deferring and ambiguity; where causality does not necessarily lie in the obvious calculus of the abstract but frequently 'in the often despised sedimentation of temporal circumstances'.[8] In what follows I have attempted to examine some of the spaces between some of these signs, dialogues and histories, and to scan the circuits in which they move and acquire significance. What emerges is not 'authentic' to any single point of origin, explanation or metaphysical axiom, but seeks rather to be authentic to a particular set of historical circumstances and associated possibilities: to the complex fabric of social and historical experience, to the (con)temporary, that is mortal, hence unique, set of conditions in which we act and make sense of our lives.

Today, we can perhaps talk in terms of a shift or reorganization of sense, a change in what Raymond Williams would have called the contemporary 'structure of feeling'. Knowledge, at least as it has been articulated in western societies, has consistently invoked optics and an ocular conception of cognizance. It has been organized via visual metaphors. As it is defined in *The Oxford Dictionary of English Etymology*, the term theory comes from the Greek *theoría* – contemplation, speculation, sight, formed on *theorós* – spectator, formed on *thea*, base of *théa* – sight, contemplation. The metaphor betrays its metaphysical lineage. It takes us all the way back to Plato's cave and its allegory of knowledge as something divined from the passing shadows on its walls, from chained beings meditating on an optical illusion, a speculum. But such representations are not about mere mimesis; what we see is coded and therefore involves not only displaying certain things but also hiding other things. In inscribing a woman's voice in the allegory Luce Irigaray brings to light the masculine partiality that passes for a fixed and universal illumination. The cave, the given, the matrix, the uterus, the hole in the Earth, provides the silent scene of representation, the space of the simulation, the: 'Eternal archive of the Idea. An infinitely delayed birth for which every diversity, every controversy, is obliterated in blind contemplation'.[9] Representation involves repression: some things are shown, other are hidden; some things said, other unsaid. For in every representation the object represented is initially cancelled and then replaced, re-presented, in another context and language.[10] Representation, as Freud noted, is a 'cannibalistic discourse', it devours and '"takes the place" of the history lost to it.'[11]

Inaugurated by the modern impact of photography and cinema, we are today in the midst of a radical permutation in our sense of vision. It involves a modification that may turn out to be as significant for how we understand the world as the introduction of geometrical perspective during the Renaissance. The referent, as encountered in the formal semblance of painting, or the photographic and cinematic image, has educated our eye to observe objects and everyday details in a certain manner. This particular organization of matter, this sense of perspective (and position), has increasingly been supplemented and then radically modified by techniques, which are never merely 'technical', in which the languages of representations are themselves increasingly foregrounded. In this marriage of technique and logos it is increasingly the syntax of such languages, rather than their referentiality, that proposes a further mutation in perspective. We increasingly find ourselves dealing less with the referential premises of a particular image and more with its languages of gestation, with its languages of becoming, with its morpho-genesis.[12] This is as true of the self-referring meditations of twentieth-century avant garde art, contemporary fashion and music as it is, for example, of the syntax of the computer. Inside the simulating machine, on the other side of the screen, there are no fixed images, no finished sounds, no final text. What we find instead are bits of information, digits of promised pitches, patterns of potential expression: shadowy traces, images of a composite world, languages of potential sense.

This, for the computer itself is also a contemporary allegory, suggests a remarkable renovation in terms of space, time, sense, and knowledge. What this 'crisis in representation' has done is to add contemporary weight to an older idea that it is the mediation, the employment and deployment of languages, rather than the objects they supposedly represent, that becomes central, that, as Wittgenstein put it, mark the limits of our world.[13] This frees individual signs from their earlier regimes of reference in a particular time, place and tradition. The more a sound, style, object or image is reproduced, quoted, sampled and referred to, whether it is the skyline of New York, or the voice of James Brown, the more an 'aura' accumulates around it. The more languages that are invested in the sign, the more 'authentic' it becomes. Walter Benjamin's original argument has been turned inside-out, as it were; it is no longer the grainy texture of the *original* painting, voice or object that draws us into a history and a tradition, but the secular and social quantity of subsequent reproductions (in prints, records, photographs, cassettes, fashion, advertising, cinema) that now guarantees a historical presence and reproduces an aura: 'we've read the signs, seen the people snapping the pictures. We can't get outside the aura. We're part of the aura. We're here, we're now.'[14] It is no longer the object but the encounter with the languages and discourses that orbit around it that counts.

It is language itself that has become both the palimpsest and fulcrum, not only of immediate sense and æsthetics, but also of an effective ethics and politics. It is the languages of pleasure, of tragedy, of pain, of hope, of freedom, of detail and difference, of death and beginning, . . . of the 'real', and not naked reality, that address us and which we, in turn, address. Thus these languages are not autonomous. They are integral to the 'social construction of reality'. Their power lies precisely in their detailed exchange with what is being continually addressed and constructed through the dialogue itself: our particular sense of time and place. In this way, our very understanding of reality becomes a political issue. For language, while representing an insuperable limit in our description of the world simultaneously involves our in-scription. 'Description never reduces the complexity of the world *but adds to it*.'[15]

Such a shift in emphasis from interpretations of a presumably already given reality to one that we come to construct and modify through the languages at our disposal is not reducible to one or other of the two dialogic poles: language or the 'real'. It is only guaranteed by the social and historical horizons that have permitted and continue to permit such a dialogue to take place.

In Ridley Scott's film *Blade Runner* (1982) there occurs a dialogue of this type set in the near future Los Angeles of 2019. One possible reading of this film is as a sci-fi parable on the ruins of western metaphysics, in which an abstract project, here pursued in the name of 'science' and technology, seeks to dominate, control and construct the 'real'. The Tyrell Corporation, headed by a Howard Hughes type recluse, constructs perfect humanoids that are used for space travel and dangerous activities in the off-world colonies. Indistinguishable from 'natural' men and women – 'more human than human is the motto of the Tyrell Corporation' – the only distinction, apart from their physical perfection, lies in the humanoids' fail-safe four year life span. However, a group of them have rebelled, captured a spaceship and returned to earth. They must be hunted down and destroyed. But finding them, the job of the 'blade runner', is no easy task. The city is complex, frustrat-ingly opaque, a labyrinth of ethnicities and tongues; its language – 'cityspeak' – a confusing metropolitan 'dub' of Japanese, English, German and Spanish. It is a reality dominated by signs of the 'other' (Asiatic, Hispanic . . .), by signs of a break-down in both an obvious urban order and in nature itself. Everything is simulated. Minerva, the owl of history that takes flight at dusk, is artificial, a construction, just like our histories, our memories, and those of the replicants in the film. In all this confusion where does the human conclude and the artificial commence, what is real and what is simulated, who is 'original' and who is a copy? We discover a world without guarantees; a world of pathos that rests on the fact that 'Unless you're alive you can't play'. And if we listen carefully to the renegade band of replicants what we hear is the ardent and ancient demand for more than their planning foresaw: more time, more life.

This sense of language as the ever present matrix in which sense is encountered and constructed and into which we are cast (in the sense of both thrown and formed: Heidegger, Lacan), also suggests the impossibility of a neat break from the murmur, echoes and voices of previous idioms and dialogues. Here there is no linear supersession of earlier contradictions. There is no *Aufhebung* in the Hegelian-Marxist sense, no linear progression or logic carrying us directly into the future, away from yesterday.[16] Rather, what can be proposed is a putative shift or movement that is not beyond and away from the past but rather involves a circulating back on it, a return, a stepping back down into its details, earlier silences and margins, into its previously 'blank' spaces and hidden networks, in order to extract from it a more extensive sense of the possible. Putting it in metaphysical terms, we can say that the struggle is not over an absolute truth, the horrifying void of the ultimate referent, in the end death, but over what is 'good' and beneficial for us.

Instead of stable foundations and a rational directive accompanying us on our journey down the single road of truth towards the 'real', we seek our liberation in the multiple voices, languages, her- and his-stories, of a world that is altogether less guaranteed, but for that lighter, more open, accessible and, in a profoundly secular sense, more possible.[17]

The impossibility of fully comprehending the world, of reducing it to a single, rational order of communication (that sought by Habermas, for example) is not necessarily a methodological defect or cultural defeat. For it leaves us free to acknowledge an irreducible heterogeneity. The monologue of a totalizing theory, is replaced by a continual dialogue across the 'hard surfaces' and 'local knowledge' of these differences, where analysis does not represent the closure of the Truth, but an attempted exchange conducted in good faith and with a certain scepticism towards its own language and position.[18] For just as we can choose to ignore the naïvety of considering language a neutral means of expression, as though it were a potential expressway to reality, so we can also choose to be suspicious of the powers claimed for it in the Nietzschean tradition. This means to remain precariously in the balance, conversing between the realist and the æsthetic extremes, between the world as a fixed presence, an open book requiring only the appropriate tools to be read, and the world as a fluctuating fiction and hermeneutic text, that can be continually deconstructed, rewritten and invented anew merely by our will to meaning and power.

It is also in the perpetual dialogue between such poles – between nature considered as the essence of 'reality', and the world perceived fundamentally as a social construction – that there exists the intellectual wager of the natural sciences. Following Roy Bhaskar, we can say that the moon would continue to orbit around the earth, the tides continue to turn, and the solar system to travel through the universe, even if there were not women and men to observe these phenomena and work up such observations into scientific tendencies and 'laws'.[19] On the other hand, the 'paradigms' (T. S. Kuhn) of sense available in the transitory dimension of the social world are altogether less securely anchored. In a later work Bhaskar himself argues that the social sciences, as cultural and historical constructions, imbricated in the very events they propose to explain, involve a subject to subject (or, concept to concept) relationship, rather than a subject–object one, and this, as the hermeneutic tradition also insists, involves 'a pre-interpreted reality, a reality already brought under concepts by social actors, that is a reality *already brought under the same kind of material in terms of which it is to be grasped* (which is the only possible medium of its intelligibility).'[20] In other words, the analysis of social reality is subject to the same languages, histories, possibilities and uncertainties that constitute our being in the world.

Social and cultural sense, then, becomes not a goal but a discourse, not a closure but a trace in an endless passage that can only aspire to a temporary arrest, to a self-conscious drawing of a limit across the diverse possibilities of the world. As Gilles Deleuze puts it, sense is a surface-effect, an event, and not the sign or symptom of an absent origin, a lost totality, or a pure consciousness.[21] It is precisely this lack of fixed referent or stable foundation that produces meaning. For to produce it does not mean to touch a sacred stone or turn the right key that will reveal the nature of things, but involves tracing out a recognizable shape on the extensive complexity of the possible. Our interpretations of society, culture, history and our individual lives, hopes, dreams, passions and sensations, involve attempts to *confer* sense rather than to *discover* it. For it is we – with our histories, languages, memories and constraints – who make sense. We never arrive at the bottom of things: the analysis remains open. Our constructions are destined to be incomplete, interminable. It is in that historical process – in the passage of time *and* being – that there lies our only chance of redemption. Though, of course, this redemption, as Adorno once pointed out, is both a mirage and a contradiction. How can we be redeemed from ourselves? To refuse the idea of a reconciled totality removes the possibility of being redeemed. Perhaps the dream of redemption can only reveal that in the end we are destined to live without (or beyond) it.

Finally, a word on the character of the essays themselves. Some readers may object to their apparent lack of discipline, to their tendency towards panoramic sweep, absence of resolution, and repetition. However, the rigour of a critical language to square what it seeks to refer to with its own metaphorical logic is won at a high price. The scepticism of the German philosopher Friedrich Nietzsche towards abstract intellectual rigour, which later re-emerges in Walter Benjamin's grappling with a 'materialist history' of nineteenth-century Paris, is deeply pertinent here, as are the discourses on the realities of the 'other' released by feminism, ethnicity and attempts to think in and through the multiple differences and specificities that constitute our world. Logic and rational clarity can paradoxically obscure more extensive, and altogether less well defined, territories.[22] Both Nietzsche and Benjamin, in considering attempts to represent the sense, the pulse, the fullness and tactile sensuousness of the world, recognized the necessity of failure. Their excessive and messianic languages were self-consciously constructed on the ruins of such a project. Since then diverse voices have been set over and against a single authority, rationalism or resolution, and have now been released into the repertoire of critical languages. There is no turning back to a simpler state. There is ultimately – Nietzschean aphorisms, Marxian critique, Freudian analysis, Benjamin's historical montage, the intricate, discursive surfing of Derrida, apart – no resolution, as Nietzsche himself persistently acknowledged. We are condemned to wander – critically, emotionally, politically . . . passionately – in a world characterized by an excess of sense which while offering the chance of meaning continues to flee ahead of us. This is our world, our responsibility, our only chance.

The reader will no doubt find much to disagree with here. That is an inevitable part of the dialogue. The intellectual referents, I imagine, are fairly obvious. The routes to them, however, may be more obscure. It is sufficient (?) to say that they emerged while living and working in and between two cultures – that of Britain and Italy – where each became the echo chamber that extended and diffused the exchange with the other. Italy has provided me with an important critical counterpoint to a British experience. It has allowed me to look back on where I came from with different eyes and ears and to unpick and reassemble some of the bits and pieces of a particular history and formation. In particular, it has offered and opened up an intellectual itinerary that, after more than a decade of 'crises' – of Marxism, of reason, of modernism – now finds me on the beach, facing that 'open sea' of critical endeavour once invoked by Nietzsche.[23] Caught between mimicry, alterity and ultimately silence, I write from two shores and between two cultures.

Chapter 2

An island life

No man is an Island, entire of itself; every man is a piece of the Continent, a part of the main.

John Donne, *Devotions XII*

In her first public speech after the ending of hostilities at Port Stanley had closed the bloody adventure in the South Atlantic (not long afterwards marketed to the public as a videocassette), Mrs Thatcher pronounced an ominous phrase: 'The lesson of the Falklands is that Britain has not changed'.

As always, the Prime Minister successfully put her finger on a contradictory but telling theme. She was personally intent on conjuring up a mystical vision from the past: that moment before the rot and decline had set in, when Britain was still 'great'. And the underlying steady-state condition to which her appeal was addressed that July afternoon in 1982 at the Cheltenham race course was destined to strike deep into the British psyche. It was designed to draw out from the twilight world of the unconscious and parade on the surfaces of the everyday the seemingly indecipherable metaphysics of 'being British'.

It may be comforting to think of the Falklands' War, Mrs Thatcher and the last decade of Conservative government rhetoric and innovation, as a temporary and unexpected rash on the British body politic. I am not so sure. It, too, is an integral part of the national tale, keen to employ a sense of the past for its version of the future. It, too, appeals to a wider sense of being, of being 'British' and being part of that particular cultural and historical reality. For this particular sense of place, belonging and tradition is also to be found in very different quarters; for example, in a radical populism and a sense of native civil rights that sees in Mrs Thatcher and her governments a real threat to Britain's democratic heritage. It is clear, then, that any attempt to decipher this appeal to 'Britishness' necessarily draws us on to a complex, contradictory and even treacherous, terrain, in which the most varied elements entwine, coexist and contaminate one another. The trope of 'Britishness' can be displaced and condensed in multiple identities, values, visions, ideas and criticisms that germinate, pollinate and take root in the soil of civil society. It is part of our differentiated cultural inheritance, part of our histories, our memories, our formation. If in the end we are forced to acknowledge that there is no obvious resolution or simple exit from this particular web then it becomes all the more important to acknowledge it and recognize its limits. Only in this manner will it perhaps become possible to live in and with it in a more knowing, open and liberated fashion.

The oldest club in the world

> Though modern constitutions typically locate the source of sovereignty in 'the people', in Britain, it is the Crown in Parliament that is sovereign. Nor is that merely a technical point. The political culture of democratic Britain assigns to ordinary people the role, not of citizens, but of subjects.
>
> R. McKenzie and A. Silver[1]

In the often turbulent narratives of modern nationalism Britain occupies a peculiar position. Although having witnessed lengthy struggles in the past, as well as in more recent, even contemporary history, to absorb internal national units – Welsh, Scots, Irish – the British Isles have not experienced a serious invasion for a millennium. Partially dismantling the feudal state in the seventeenth century, the English state was also the first in the centuries that followed to experience the fracturing impacts and fruits of industrialization, urbanization and empire. Such precedents have provided British political culture, and the particular English hegemony that lies at its heart, with a present day mantle of benevolent overseer, as it looks down on more ragged procedures, more hurried and violent constitutions.

The 'suppressed superiority' (Tom Nairn) of this English ascendancy, hidden behind a self-deprecation that is usually unwilling to admit that nationalism exists at all, clearly has its roots in the quiet certainties of this stable and largely conservative tradition. The earlier connections between radical liberties and 'Englishness' that flared up in the seventeenth, eighteenth and early nineteenth centuries have largely been extinguished and are now publicly presented as part of a placid native 'tradition'. Since the latter half of the last century such struggles over the different possibilities of patriotism have been largely replaced by a tranquillizing image in which 'Britishness' invariably stands for the quiet authority and organic continuity of a Home Counties conservatism; a settlement that is not simply political but also, and quite significantly, cultural in its effect. Symbolically elaborated around consecrated relics, traditions and shrines – Westminster, the Monarchy, Oxbridge, the Royal Navy, the public school system, the syllabus of 'English' – it is as though, through an undisturbed continuity, the very spirit of 'History' has laid its blessing on the nation.

It has also led to the successful establishment of an extensive *popular* cultural consensus. For while, historically speaking, there exists an important popular and oppositional dimension to British institutional politics, at least since the beginnings of mass franchise in 1867, it too has come increasingly to be represented in the timeless guise of a national mythology, where faithful subjects (rather than 'citizens') rally round the flag in times of crisis.[2] So, while today formally one of the least democratic of countries in the conduct of its political life, glaringly apparent in its unrepresentative electoral system, the maintenance of a non-elected House of Lords, and the powerful symbolism of its monarchy, the public image of Britain is still that of one of democracy's champions, one of its brightest jewels. On 3 April 1982, in the parliamentary debate the day after Argentinian forces had occupied the Falkland Islands, we can hear Mr Michael Foot, then leader of the Labour Party, intoning this familiar litany, claiming Britain 'to be a defender of people's freedom throughout the world'.

The seemingly uninterrupted continuity and timeless rituals of these traditions and institutions have provided the comforting guarantees. The construction of 'English' history and letters in the nineteenth century, both in the world of academia and in the literary milieu of the period, impregnated the whole debate on culture with the moral tale of this national mythology.[3] In their neo-Gothic architecture, pre-Raphaelite paintings, chivalric poetry, fourteenth-century socialist utopias, and their insistence on the earlier harmonies of rural life and artisan production, Victorian intellectuals of the most varied political persuasions sealed a pact between a mythical vision of the nation and their selection and installation of an acceptable cultural heritage. British culture, and its profound sense of 'Englishness' (the narrowing of the national nomenclature was not accidental), was found, in both the temporal and symbolic sense, to exist beyond the mechanical rhythms and commercial logic of industrial society and the modern world. It has subsequently bequeathed that deep seated intellectual and moral aversion to modernism, mass culture, and mass democracy, and a corresponding acquiescence to the authority of tradition, that has so characterized English intellectual thought and official culture in the twentieth century. In its unbending moral clarity and particular sense of history it has 'given us the map of an upright and decent country'.[4]

This perspective has recently been supplemented and renovated by the vigorous language of Mrs Thatcher and her governments. The rather crusty world of yesterday's Britain has been harnessed to a more aggressive rhythm. Victorian values are still central, but these now reflect the businesslike, utilitarian logic of that imagined epoch rather than its gloomy æsthetes and a cricket-playing, claret-drinking, *noblesse oblige*. There has occurred a shift towards an *imaginary* modernity. Imaginary, because in all its talk of financial independence, profitability and enterprise culture, the Thatcherite vision of the contemporary world is as significantly indebted to a backward-looking sense of the national heritage as the patronizing intellectual and aristocratic cultures it purports to be pragmatically reassessing.

The empires of Albion

The growth of official nationalism in Europe towards the end of the nineteenth century, together with the pomp and circumstances surrounding the Empire and the public ascent of the monarchy in late Victorian England, often served to camouflage much of British culture's deeply ambiguous relationship to the real sources of its power: industry and the formation of the modern, metropolitan state. In all this the apparently timeless language and traditions of 'Englishness' provided a source of reassuring images that in an eternal Edwardian summer shut out the change and competition of the wider world before it was all rudely shattered by world war, fascism and American hegemony.

This type of argument is certainly not new, nor necessarily restricted to radical critics and cultural analysts. It invariably occupies a central place in many of the diatribes on modern Britain's 'decline'. But, for all its obviousness, I feel that it occupies a pivotal role not merely in economic matters but also, and in some ways, more acutely, in the formation of native cultural criticism and studies. I want to try and illustrate the inherited *limits* (which are not necessarily always the same as shortcomings) of this particular tradition within the context of contemporary cultural analysis. I will start at the most obvious point, that is with the years 1956–8 and the publication of Richard Hoggart's *The Uses of Literacy* and the late Raymond Williams' *Culture and Society*. Commencing from here I want to try and draw out the role played by a strong, but rarely acknowledged, sense of 'Englishness' in this native critical tradition.

In both Williams' reconstruction of the culture and society debate between 1780 and 1950 across the key terms of 'industry', 'democracy', 'class', 'art' and 'culture', and in Hoggart's detailed representation of the relations and realities of inter-war working-class life in a northern town, there occurs an irreversible shift away from a purely elite and isolated conception of native culture. No longer considered as a restricted sphere ('high culture'), both Hoggart and Williams understood culture to involve 'a whole way of life'. There are two principal perspectives that emerge from this initial change in outlook. One, and it is this aspect that has usually been developed, examines the complex relations and clashes, particularly along class lines, that constitute this 'whole way of life'. The other possible line of enquiry, with its underlying reference to a particular social formation as a historical 'bloc', has tended to be far less developed, usually only emerging when culture is considered in terms of separate class 'unities' or in the wider but altogether vaguer framework of national traditions and 'community'. It is this second possibility that I want to look at in further detail.

A striking characteristic of British cultural studies, and this is certainly apparent in continental Europe, and, I think, also in North America, has been the conceptual centrality given to class as the point in which cultural power and expression is articulated. The post-war contributions of native Marxist historiography and then later radical sociology can be distinctly felt in this formulation. What I want here to try and suggest, without denying the valency of class in cultural formations, is the pertinence of an ultimately wider 'unity', in both its internal distinctions and common concerns, provided by a particular national formation.

In the mid-1960s, Perry Anderson and Tom Nairn published a series of articles in *New Left Review* that sought to explain the 'origins' of the British crisis.[5] To put it in the broadest terms, they located that crisis in the 'historical compromise' which they argued took place in the course of the nineteenth century between a rising industrial bourgeoisie and an established aristocracy. Almost two decades later, this thesis has been extended and further underwritten by the American historian Martin Wiener.[6] Recently Anderson himself has returned to these arguments and added a further dimension.[7]

In this latest version the argument shifts away slightly from the supposed *entente* forged between the native bourgeoisie and aristocracy (particularly because, although with different hues and tones, this has turned out to be a fairly constant feature in modern Europe), and concentrates attention on the historical time-scale of British capitalism and the peculiarities of its mode of production. What is here revealed is not so much a compromise between two social classes as a lengthy osmosis between agrarian capital and industrial development, with the former (landed wealth, interests and connections to the Court and the City) socially, culturally and economically dominating the second. The upshot was not so much the social alliance between the aristocracy and a rising, industrially-based, bourgeoisie, but the further observation that Britain never fully experienced modern capitalism. Its state, civil service and industrial plant were deeply compromised by an older political and economic settlement that witnessed landed wealth and City finance being consolidated and expanding at the price of modern industrial development and business. In other words, the historical basis of British capitalism – large, solvent, agrarian enterprises and the financial power of the City of London, which increasingly came to depend on the world, rather than its domestic economy – were laid down and they map out the contours of subsequent development well before the epoch of modern industry.[8] The latter was destined to remain a junior partner in this triad. What both hid and permitted this peculiar compromise was largely the extensive profits and protection provided by the British Empire.

Now this protective shield of Empire was not merely of economic importance, it was also of profound cultural import. I am thinking here, in particular, of how the emergence and consolidation of the Empire not only shielded British industry from capitalist competition abroad, thereby blunting subsequent native industrial development while at the same time encouraging the financial expansion of the City, but also of how it contributed to forming the economic and cultural life of subordinate social classes and cultures at home.

The historian Gareth Stedman-Jones has pointed out that it was in such a context, in a society dominated in the late nineteenth century by metropolitan London, that many of the political and cultural horizons of members of a modern, urban working class and its forms of political representation were established.[9] It produced what he has significantly characterized as a 'culture of consolation', a culture that was fundamentally pragmatic in its goals and overwhelmingly defensive. With the loss of an earlier, utopian, spirit (Owenism, Chartism), libertarian and feminist concerns were pushed right off the increasingly corporate political agenda of the day.[10] Neither religious nor socialist, it was on the whole a fatalistic culture, believing in luck and destiny, politically sceptical, debunking upper-class life, but largely accepting the existing state of affairs, escapist but strongly rooted in the everyday realities of working-class life. Here we can recognize many of the threads that make up the back-cloth of Richard Hoggart's version of working-class culture in Leeds in the 1930s. The important supplement to this picture is that social hegemony at home was supported and extended by a national superiority abroad: the British working class formed part of the 'lower classes', but it was simultaneously allied to that native hegemony in its presumed superiority over the disdainfully nicknamed populations of the Empire and the rest of the world. Friedrich Engels, writing in 1894, spoke of 'English workers with their sense of imaginary national superiority'.

It should be noted that this is not simply an argument about how the working class in an imperialist centre was 'bought off' by economically benefiting from imperialism *à la Lenin*. It is above all an argument about a particular cultural formation in which ideas, however imaginary, about nation and history, and your particular place and participation in them, act as quite real and material forces in the everyday world.[11] It was in the public spectacle, adventure, exotica and romance of the predominantly male genre of 'Empire' – fostered in hundreds of boys' comics, tea packets and cigarette cards, novels, songs, adventure stories, music hall and later cinema, along with the pageantry of monarchy and an imperial militia 'dressed to kill in bed- or ballroom; armed with swords and obsolete industrial weapons; in peace on display, in war on horseback' – that imperialism and the social darwinism of the 'white man's burden' was popularized and domesticated.[12]

It is worthwhile underlining this extensive but compact view of 'Britishness', and its repercussions on the native view of the rest of the world. For although the sun may well have set on the British Empire many of the ideas and illusions it once sustained – particularly in its stereotyped recognition of the colonial 'other' – have proved to have a remarkable after-life, in some cases continuing their zombied existence right down into the present. Further, the largely uninterrupted continuity and traditions of British civil society and state have not only permitted it to continue with some of these illusions but also with the anachronistic forms of hegemony that gestated them (although these sometimes back-fire, as in the case of Northern Ireland). Needless to say, all this has deeply affected indigenous methods of contemplating and analysing the rest of the surrounding world. It could be said to have become part of the 'national language'.

Native reason

Mock on, mock on, Voltaire, Rousseau;
Mock on, mock on; 'tis all in vain!
You throw the sand against the wind,
And the wind blows it back again.

And every sand becomes a gem
Reflected in the beams divine;
Blown back they blind the mocking eye,
But still in Israel's paths they shine.

The Atoms of Democritus
And Newton's Particles of Light
Are sands upon the Red Sea shore,
Where Israel's tents do shine so bright.

William Blake, *Mock on, mock on, Voltaire, Rousseau*

This optimistic Blakean vision of reason, religion and democracy, where Albion is identified with the destiny of Israel and
humankind ('Was Britain the primitive seat of the Patriarchal
Religion? . . . "All things begin and end in Albion's ancient
Druid rocky shore."', *Jerusalem*), although cast into more
sceptical and mystical verse in the poet's later years, provides a
fitting epigram to modern English reasoning. For if there is a
mode of thought that both British intellectual life and its
everyday culture share it is the moral faith in empiricism. In
asking ourselves why this might be the case we are drawn into
observing that the foundations of what is called modernity
were laid down many centuries ago, in the English case even
before the rationalist explosion of the European Enlightenment. Crucial here was the massive process of secularization
induced by the Reformation and the Scientific Revolution,
when 'knowledge' was literally brought down to earth.
Without going into the details of the sceptical rationalism of
Bishop Berkeley and the Scottish philosopher David Hume,
and their proposal to equate knowledge with the immediacy of
sense data, it is perhaps just sufficient to note that the
seventeenth century triumph of science in British intellectual
life, that was to be publicly extended in the following
centuries, in particular in the figure of Charles Darwin,
seemingly provided a fundamental endorsement to an empirical mode of knowledge. Knowledge was constituted by what

could be reported, observed, measured and classified. It was, of course, further supported by the very mechanics of the Industrial Revolution where what appeared to be the direct application of scientific principles to nature were literally remaking the world. In this context an ideology of empirical pragmatism could, and was, erected: the world was to be continually 'tested' and 'verified', not by a theory, but by an empirical intelligence. Knowledge is constructed in what you can touch, sense, feel and physically transform.

Hume's position – that knowledge is ultimately dependent upon experience – was eventually refuted by the German philosopher Immanuel Kant in his *Critique of Pure Reason* (1781); Kant's argument freed the field of knowledge from being limited to sense experience. He argued that although all knowledge begins with experience it does not follow that it all arises out of experience. This opened up the possibility of treating knowledge as a field in its own right, and offered the further prospect of constructing a mental schema or structure for interpreting the world. This takes us to the Continent, back to Giambattista Vico, and then forward to Hegel, to Marx and Marxism, and to the whole continental tradition that is willing to think in terms of structures, totalities and overt metaphysics. But all this developed elsewhere, largely in Germany, and obviously represents a quite different trajectory of thought and conceptualization of knowledge from that pursued in Britain.

The development of a particular British cultural formation that was empirical and therefore deeply tied to a pragmatic view of things was, apart from the existence of the Industrial Revolution, greatly assisted by the particular insularity of the British national experience in the nineteenth century, cut off, as it was, from the rest of the world by the buffer and the barrier of its Empire. In fact, it seemed, and many Britons in their 'splendid isolation' would have concurred, as though Britain was the 'world'. Everything else was simply 'foreign' and 'strange'.

What needs to be underlined here is that the successful and largely unchallenged establishment of an empirical mode of thought led away from any temptation to indulge in the construction of an intellectual or theoretical totality. If the world is composed of millions of empirical situations, it can be catalogued, but not captured in a single a priori theory or

overriding explanation, with the crucial exception of the mind
of God. In this perspective, theories are just the accumulative
and organizational frameworks of so many facts that make up
an ultimately knowable world. It involves an implicit and
unacknowledged metaphysics of its own – the stable referent
of an irrefutable and independently verifiable world – that was
usually displaced into the apparently neutral language of
'science' and 'learning'.

This drive to verify and possess the world comes to its
conclusion on the Victorian high ground that sought 'to make
the independent individual the ground of value'.[13] Here, too,
religion was also based on the sovereign individual's experience of sense data. For Matthew Arnold there was no space for
miracles and mysticism: 'Whatever is to stand must rest upon
something which is verifiable, not unverifiable'.[14] T. H. Huxley
praised Hume's attack on metaphysics which, now supported
by nineteenth-century physical sciences, was 'warranted to
drive solid bolts of fact through the thickest skulls'.[15]

Such a prospect is not only empirical, it is also imperial.
Everything falls within its domain and is susceptible to its
immediate rule. This conception of knowledge, further encouraged in the latter half of the nineteenth century by a positivist
view of science, was extensively endorsed by the very real
economic, political and cultural sense of the nation and the
cultural projection of 'Britishness' that established itself at
home and abroad in the second half of the nineteenth century.
The native manner of looking at and understanding the world
was the unique way. This local 'common sense', whose
gendered and ethnic constructions were easily obscured
beneath the neutrality of empirical data, has invariably
suggested a secure belief in what constitutes 'knowledge' and
meaning. But, for all its bluff pragmatism and endorsement of
the 'facts', the Victorian attempt to continually establish a
moral ground does at times hint at a deeper, underlying
insecurity; the neurotic suspect that behind the rational *ratio* of
the world there lay in its 'heart of darkness' perhaps altogether
more disquieting realities: other, more dangerous, worlds.

This complex inheritance of empiricism and imperialism is
deeply ingrained in the English 'structure of feeling'. Even
without further analysis there is the contemporary intuition
that questions of race and racism, the 'Empire strikes back' as a

book title put it some years ago, along with the widespread disdain for intellectuals and theory in British public life, share some common roots in this particular story.[16] Meanwhile, the striking insularity and parochialism of much of British academia, pragmatically wedded to collecting the 'facts' and observing 'reality', has tended to produce a 'naturalist' art and an empiricist intelligentsia.[17] For what is ultimately significant about the mythology of the transparent factuality of the world is what it hides, forbids and represses. Behind its languages of neutral representation lies a deeply ingrained and apprehensive moralism, itself a powerful legacy of a patrician culture accustomed to the quiet and pragmatic exercise of its authority in the belief that it can somehow fully explain things.

The man in the white suit

Some of the most radical criticism coming out of the West today is the result of an interested desire to conserve the subject of the West, or the West as Subject.

Gayatri Chakravorty Spivak[18]

It is there, in the colonial margin, that the culture of the west reveals its 'différance', its limit-text, as its practice of authority displays an ambivalence that is one of the most significant discursive and psychical strategies of discriminatory power – whether racist or sexist, peripheral or metropolitan.

Homi K. Bhabha[19]

What we always forget is that the overwhelming bulk of the British proletariat does not live in Britain, but in Asia and Africa.

George Orwell in 1939[20]

In his examination of the trial of Warren Hastings in 1788 for crimes and 'misdemeanours' committed while Governor-General of India between 1773 and 1784, David Musselwhite points to 'the confrontation of systems of thought and cultural codings and expectations which are completely impenetrable to each other and which encourage us, therefore, to try and imagine what it would be like to think the "unthinkable".'[21] There occurs the crucial clash, as Musselwhite goes on to establish, with Hastings' principal accuser, Philip Francis, 'imposing Enlightenment and European principles of political economy on India while, on the other, Hastings is concerned to manipulate as best he can the residual machinery of the Moghul Empire.'[22]

Although Hastings was formally acquitted, he was nevertheless morally condemned in the emerging daily press and popular opinion of the day. There, a native sense of values triumphed over the detailed knowledge and diplomacy that Hastings had exercised in dealing with Islamic law. As Homi Bhabha puts it:

> Colonial power produces the colonized as a fixed reality which is at once an 'other' and yet entirely knowable and visible. It resembles a form of narrative in which the productivity and circulation of subjects and signs are bound in a reformed and recognizable totality. It employs a system of representation, a regime of truth, that is structurally similar to realism.[23]

It was the constructed, and deeply 'English', view of 'India', rather than a respectful, local working knowledge, that was marshalled by Francis, Burke and others seeking to have Hastings impeached. It was a myth, and one that clearly worked at home. It produced an 'India' that was both different but yet finally susceptible to domestication. What is being denied here 'is any knowledge of cultural otherness as a differential *sign*, implicated in specific historical and discursive conditions, requiring construction in different practices or reading.'[24] Such a recognition would lead to the dispersal of the logic that fails to recognize 'otherness' in its fullness and for which 'otherness' is merely a corroboration, a point on the other side of the circle that completes the logo-centrism of the discourse (colonial, imperialist, male, hegemonic) in question. For racial and cultural 'otherness' does not complete the circle, it circulates and proliferates in the world in the 'spiral of différance'.[25] There it marks a difference and defers or postpones an obvious resolution.

This specific argument interestingly links up, and it is hardly accidental, to the important philosophical work on 'otherness' by the Jewish philosopher Emmanuel Lévinas. In his book, *Totality and Infinity*, Lévinas argues against traditional metaphysics for 'reducing the Other to the Same'. He points out that singular bodies appear merely as 'individuals' against a total background which renders them comprehensible only to the degree that they refer to that totality. The totality is what the knowing subject already knows prior to encountering such bodies, and such bodies being referred to the already noted or known are not recognized as such, but are immediately reduced to the Same, to the knowing subject.[26]

In a similar vein, Bhabha points to how the colonial subject is constructed within

> an apparatus of power which *contains*, in both senses of the word, an 'other' knowledge: a knowledge that is arrested and fetishistic and circulates through colonial discourses that limited form of otherness, that fixed form of difference, that I have called the stereotype.'[27]

To conclude and to bring home this argument on Anglo-centric representation/realism: 'It is as if the very emergence of the "colonial" is dependent for its representation upon some strategic limitation or prohibition *within* the authoritative discourse itself . . . in which to be Anglicized, is emphatically not to be English.'[28]

Here, today, we face the possibility of two perspectives and two versions of 'Britishness'. One, is Anglo-centric, frequently conservative, backward-looking, and increasingly located in a frozen and largely stereotyped idea of the national, that is English, culture. The other is ex-centric, open-ended and multi-ethnic. The first is based on a homogeneous 'unity' in which history, tradition and individual biographies and roles, including ethnic and sexual ones, are fundamentally fixed and embalmed in the national epic, in the mere fact of being 'English'. The other perspective suggests an overlapping network of histories and traditions, a heterogeneous complexity in which positions and identities, including that of the 'national', cannot be taken for granted, and are not interminably fixed but tend towards flux.

In the construction of the nation as an 'imagined community', to use Benedict Anderson's term, we discover that 'race' is clearly a social and political construction; it is not simply something to do with the colour of our skin.[29] For while colour is a loaded signifier, an ethnic signal, it stands in for a whole range of meanings: linguistic, historical and cultural. In the end we are dealing with cultural identity and with what is usually an attempt to hold at bay the disrupting and transgressive presence of the 'other'; we are dealing with a particular definition of 'Britishness', of being one of 'us', as opposed to one of 'them', rather than simply with the labelling of skin pigment on the colour spectrum.

So, for example, black or Asian people can be acceptable to Mrs Thatcher and much of the Conservative party if they respect a particular sense of 'Britishness', that is if they dress, talk, eat and act as native-born Britons. It is this tradition that they are expected to enter and uphold, which correspondingly implies that they negate their own particular histories: imperial, colonial, racial, ethnic, cultural and religious. They are expected to become the mirror of a homogeneous, white Britain; the invisible men and women of the black diaspora and the post-colonial world who are required to mimic their allotted roles in the interpretative circle to which they have been assigned.[30]

This Anglo-centric, and self-referring, position is based on a homogeneous 'unity' in which particular roles, including gender, are firmly established. In the present attempted revival of Victorian values it recalls not the liberal aristocrat but the sombre virtues and rational order of the rising middle class whose personal capacities were realized in a moral relationship to the market and to domesticity.[31] Mrs Thatcher's appeal here is to a vague, but potent, symbol of national mythology. The details of her inspiration are even more revealing however. In her research on the articulation of 'Britishness' through ethnicity and gender, Catherine Hall has charted an important shift in middle-class English male culture that emerges around the mid-nineteenth century.[32] The English 'gentleman' of the time was not tied initially to land but was rather associated with the early nineteenth-century European trinity of Romanticism, evangelicism and political economy. In his firm belief in Christian manliness and femininity, and the insistence on this gendered distinction through the division between public life and domesticity, this male figure represented a moral critique, organized around the dignity of labour and its independent realization in the market, of aristocratic degeneracy and effeminacy.

But from his sturdy assurance in the market-place this Victorian gentleman gradually succumbed to a neo-romantic, increasingly anti-market and anti-industrial ethos. Moral certitude, and an individual and pragmatic rationale, gave way to the collective mystique of the nation and its past – 'haunts of ancient peace' – in which questions of ethics were effectively translated into questions of ethnicity. To be 'British', was no longer to demonstrate Christian virtues and the pragmatic pursuits of *homo economicus*, but to pledge allegiance to the imagined state of grace which was the nation. As the wife of the protagonist in Alexander Korda's imperialist adventure film *The Four Feathers* (1939) neatly puts it: 'we are not free, we are born in a tradition, there is a code we must respect; we must obey in order to be proud of ourselves.'[33]

By the 1860s, liberalism, *laissez-faire* culture and individual morality was giving way to life on the North-West frontier, the British Bulldog and popular racism.[34] The nation is expressed in racially exclusive terms, and the connection between it and native 'manhood', formed in the zenith of imperialism, was to be extended even further by vulgar Darwinism and metropolitan power. This has all been subsequently articulated through the long history of twentieth-century post-imperial decline, providing a repertoire of common sense and racial stereotyping capable of explaining Britain's position in the contemporary world. Talking of the provincial xenophobia revealed in present-day football riots and hooliganism, for example, John Williams has this to say:

These trends, despite the indignant protestations of politicians, are not alien to or isolated from those more widely held in British society. They are apparent, for example, in our daily news coverage of local and foreign affairs and in the violent rantings of parliamentary spokespeople for 'revenge' on the terrace gangs. The Rambo-like xenophobia of such fans, their anti-intellectualism and racism and their Page Three sexism may be forged in mean streets and massaged by the popular rags, but such values also echo way beyond these dark passages.[35]

Of course, through the mists of time, both the earlier, dissenting, evangelical, romantic, liberal movement and its subsequent metamorphosis into Bulldog Drummond and blustering certitude, can be quietly telescoped into a common, national heritage, distinguished not by challenge, change and transformation, but by a continuity guaranteed through the undisturbed ethnicity of the nation.[36] Others are welcomed to join, but on condition that they accept this narrow platform. Here, to be 'British', even though the Empire has physically gone, is somehow still to be spiritually and morally at the centre of the world.

Englishness: a moral economy

One of the significant characteristics of the Victorian city was its widespread abandonment by the spokespersons of culture. It was, significantly, the æsthetically re-invested and physically re-built Paris, rather than a forsaken London, that Walter Benjamin nominated 'capital of the nineteenth century'.[37] When the English urban world was explored the reports that came back were invariably couched in deeply pessimistic tones: the modern city represented the obvious antithesis not merely of culture, but of humanity itself. Dickens's 'Coketown' (*Hard Times*), and Gissing's 'abysses of the nether world' (*The Nether World*), provided the occasion for veritable sermons against the degeneracy and despair of the modern urban experience. They form part of a long line of secure, moral judgements that, running from the Romantics and Thomas Carlyle down to the Leavises, were to provide much of the stern backbone of the native 'culture and society' tradition.

The fascination of Edgar Allen Poe's 'man of the crowd', and the amoral dalliance and researched æstheticism of Baudelaire's *flâneur*, was to find little echo in the morally restrictive vision of their contemporaries in Britain. It is significant that the physical and æsthetic shock of the modern city suggested by Poe and, above all, Baudelaire, was ultimately to prove central to the formation of Walter Benjamin's æsthetics, in particular to his arguments on the distracted reception and tactile appropriation of modern culture, and thus to his projected study of Paris.[38] As a further historical footnote, it is worthwhile noting that Baudelaire's own *flâneur* style was inspired by an earlier English dandyism: *le vrai chic anglais*.

He tried to appear (as it had been Delacroix's aim to appear) a *vrai Gentleman*, and fascinated by the dandyism of Beau Brummel he made of that exquisite a sort of philosophical principle. English simplicity was the essence of his costume, as his black coat, brown trousers, and polished pumps bore witness, and he would even use sandpaper in order to remove the vulgar bloom of newness.[39]

Native certitude, coupled to a cultural aversion to industry, and a deeply ambiguous reaction to the prospects of mass democracy, perhaps helps to explain why the potential openings of modernism – the philosophy of experimentation and the 'new' – were largely destined to develop on the margins, if not completely outside official British culture. The initially foreign, predominantly French, impetus of early modernism – from Baudelaire and Flaubert to Impressionism – was largely introduced into British circles by the American Whistler and the Irishmen George Moore and Oscar Wilde. It was, after all, between the periphery of then metropolitan Britain (Dublin) and *Mitteleuropa* (Trieste) that the modern *Ulysses* was written, while *The Waste Land* was the work of an ex-philosophy student from the United States.[40] Apart from the brief period of Vorticism just before the First World War – the vortography of Alvin Langdon Coburn, Epstein's sculptures, the works of Wyndham Lewis, the magazine *Blast* ('Review of the Great London Vortex') – the modern avant-garde as it developed in Cubism, Futurism and Surrealism largely remained an extraneous experience for twentieth-century Britain.[41]

For modernism represented a dangerous dialogue. It is a term that has been used to cover a wide variety of historical and æsthetic tendencies.[42] It stands in for both a historical epoch and for a multiple set of movements in the arts that spans the nineteenth and twentieth centuries in Europe and North America. But although composed of many strands its cultural drift, in both the historical and artistic sense, can be said to fall into the orbit of industrialism, urbanization, mass culture and mass democracy. Here *modernism* signifies an imperative sense of time, and a corresponding mobile æsthetics, a fascination with the unknown in which a shifting mosaic of proposals are gathered together under the rubric of what Harold Rosenberg once rather paradoxically called 'the tradition of the new'. But, at the same time, modernism has also frequently involved attempts to articulate a rational and coherent vision of the world, that is to enter into the novelty of the unknown in order to curb it and set a limit. Here it repeatedly finds itself involved in a self-conscious dialogue with a dangerous 'other'. For on the other side of its constructed order lie the unordered discontents of civilization – the extremes of artistic expression, the urban masses, the colonial subject, the subaltern cultures and individuals it does not represent, its 'unconscious', an excess – which threaten its stability with dissidence and decadence, nonsense and nihilism.

That particular side of modernism eventually entered British culture largely through another route: that of a widely despised urban, commercial, popular culture. It was through the appropriation of distinctive foreign cultures and tastes, drawn from the cinema, dances and leisure styles of North America, from Afro-American music, from Continental fashion, and more recently from the fragmented inheritance of an imperial past brought home to the metropolitan centre by post-colonial migration, that a different sense of 'Britishness' has managed to both historically and æsthetically establish itself.

The paradox, but well kept secret, was that what made the earlier abandonment of both the city and much of the 'modern' experience possible was the wealth and space generated by the Industrial Revolution and the Empire. The city had been forsaken for the timeless sanctuary of the country, which, if you could not actually live there could be recreated in miniature in the simulacrum of the English garden.[43] This is the suburban solution to rural mythology, where class, gender and domesticity entwine in a miniature Eden and discover an edifying lifestyle among the potted plants, offered in John Loudon's *The Suburban Gardener and Villa Companion*, published in 1838. Meanwhile, the real countryside was simultaneously re-presented in rustic and recreational panoramas. Working figures largely disappear from view, and the meanness and misery of rural life is generally obscured by a tranquil pastoralism. Symbolically transformed into an empty landscape in the canvases of Constable and Gainsborough, the countryside provided a suitably placid metaphor, once the potential disturbance of agricultural labourers and the rural poor had been literally removed from the picture, for an abstractly conceived national culture.[44] It offered a world neatly separated from the dirty, utilitarian logic of industry and commerce; a world in which it became possible to imagine the lost community and real nature of 'Britishness'.

When William Morris, in *The Dream of John Ball*, proposed a socialist society, the model he offered was not post-capitalist, but pre-, located in the harmony of a medieval village and an artisan mode of production. Fifty years later, the Leavises in Cambridge sought to establish the nation's 'great tradition' around the literary image of seventeenth-century England. Meanwhile Evelyn Waugh revisited the British aristocracy and J. B. Priestley toured a part of the nation in his *English Journey* (1934), and both discovered in antique stones, lanes, hills and country houses the true source of England's culture. In their very different ways, these are all views based on a shared reaction to industry, urbanization and the modern world.

Under the long shadows of the Empire, which had for so long shielded Britain from the direct blast of modern capitalism and competition, a national, and prevalently nostalgic, myth of 'Englishness', usually located in the countryside, but everywhere tied to the stable logic of tradition and community, grew up. It permitted the initial Romantic distinction between art and industry, and its subsequent refinement during the nineteenth century in the debate between culture and the emergence of urban democracy, to continue unchallenged for so long. Clearly, what this has bequeathed to the present goes far beyond the more obvious tokens of an anti-industrial pastoralism, in which the 'natural and the national' are so deeply entwined, and which is so evident in the contemporary British heritage industry, in Tolkien's Middle Earth, or Richard Adams' bunny rabbit epic *Watership Down*.[45]

In this sheltered and bucolic world, ideas about English culture have invariably been associated with the concept of organic community and an accompanying sense of 'authenticity'. It is the latter, with its credulous references to the timeless realm of the 'natural', and an empirical understanding of knowledge, that has persistently provided the ultimate yardstick for so many native æsthetic, moral *and* political views. The preferred *locus* was the rural community, but it could also be extended, as, for example, in the case of George

Orwell and Richard Hoggart, to include a later, urban variant.[46] It was the idea of culture as being the natural outgrowth or product of tradition, stamped by local and, although implicit, this is mentioned less often, ethnic identities, that subsequently created a common vision of the lost worlds of the community and nation. The epochs and time-scales employed – that of Shakespearean England or the 'traditional' urban, working class of the late-nineteenth and early twentieth century – were often wildly divergent, but the desire was uniform. And where this consensus was most significantly revealed was, as Dick Hebdige has shown, in a common condemnation of contemporary 'mass culture': in its very un-English 'modernism' and distinctly 'foreign', styles, tastes, organization and æsthetics.[47]

At this point I think that two details emerge. One is that the native cultural debate, where æsthetic concerns almost invariably slide into firm moral categories, involved a complex and sometimes contorted response not only to mass culture, but also to mass democracy. The other, and related aspect, is of how modernism in both the arts and in everyday life was generally perceived as a 'foreign' threat. Whether this was represented by the Continental avant-garde, or simply by the wider and more imprecise menace of the speed and slickness of 'Americanization', it was something to be confidently identified as distinctly 'un-British'. Even the 1951 Festival of Britain, ostensibly a centenary celebration of industrial triumph – the Great Exhibition of 1851 – and the hopes of post-war modernity, was tellingly presented in the Official Guide Book as a 'Landscape'. The exhibition was laid out in a series of 'chapters' that offered a 'natural' unrolling of the national narrative.[48]

As the modern world crept up on Britain the possibility of dropping it all and escaping abroad was seriously considered. After the Great War, the Empire adventure was no longer so alluring as it was updated into the more modern, but altogether less exotic concept of the Commonwealth. For exploration, adventure and the raw immediacy of the natural you had to seek out the forgotten corners of the world: like D. H. Lawrence establishing an 'authentic' communion with the cosmos in the desert of New Mexico, or else search for an eleventh-century tower along the frontier between Persia and

Afghanistan, or plunge, in *Boy's Own* style, into the Amazonian and West African jungle.[49] This was the period of the British literary emigration: Lawrence, Douglas, Isherwood, Huxley, Auden, Greene, Orwell, Waugh. It was also the moment when some of the ground rules of future tourism were inadvertently laid down. There was the whole social and cultural re-evaluation of exposure to the sun; there were Continental express trains, and the inauguration of the Mediterranean temples of Italy and the French Riviera. But all this was not yet tourism, not yet mass holidaying, but rather the more noble art of travel.

The desire for another world was linked to the continuing refusal of industrial culture and urban life. England is abandoned, its food and weather ridiculed. As George Bowling in Orwell's *Coming up for Air* (1939) describes his eating of a frankfurter in a London milk-bar: 'It gave me the feeling that I'd bitten into the modern world', and, predictably enough, he found it horrible. Paul Fussell rightly points out that the literature represented by these inter–war writers can be read as 'a rhetorical critique of industrialism; they are prosecuting a perhaps more richly dramatized and lyricized continuation of the complaints of Ruskin, Arnold and Morris.'[50] 'Authenticity' is, once again, the key word here; it is a value, a morality to be opposed to the felt degradation of the contemporary world. But it is a value that is no longer expressed in the confident tones of an Arnold or a Ruskin: everything has now become a little less certain. This, after all, is the epoch of mass culture, mass democracy and mass warfare, the world can no longer be so easily moulded to fit a finely-turned phrase or opinion.

At home, the moral and measuring tone of English was being self-consciously developed in literary criticism by F. R. and Q. D. Leavis at Cambridge in the 1930s and 1940s in the pages of the journal *Scrutiny*. In their pursuit and identification of the literary canon, the Leavises sought out a literature that was close to the experience and feelings of a 'community' and its 'tradition'. It was those texts which permitted this communication that constituted the 'great tradition' – the conceptual guide to a native genius and its moral soul. 'This criticism was, therefore, a form of intuitionism: specifically, it consisted in *the intuition of moral values in literary experience.*'[51] The reduction of 'culture' to the morality of 'English' and the literary canon is unambiguously spelled out by F. R. Leavis himself in *Mass Civilization and Minority Culture* (1930):

> In any period it is upon a very small minority that the discerning appreciation of art and literature depends. . . . The minority capable not only of appreciating Dante, Shakespeare, Donne, Baudelaire, Hardy (to take major instances) but of recognizing their latest successors constitute the consciousness of the race (or of a branch of it) at a given time. . . . Upon them depend the implicit standards that order the finer living of an age, the sense that this is worth more than that, this rather than that is the direction in which to go, that the centre is here rather than there. In their keeping . . . is the language, the changing idiom, upon which fine living depends, and without which distinction of spirit is thwarted and incoherent. By 'culture' I mean the use of such a language. [52]

This, then, was the cultivated response to the novel flux of the modern world where culture apparently faced the threat of being confused and contaminated by the crowds and commerce of industry and the city. Before such a prospect culture was evoked to establish a quality that existed beyond the vulgar tangibility of everyday life. Its values were considered to be timeless, somehow perpetually 'true': the great novels, the great plays, paintings and poems. Art and culture, uncontaminated by the mean forces of the immediate world, was the repository of such values. It is literature – the 'best' that has been thought and written, in Matthew Arnold's words – that then becomes the measure of the world, the moral ruler of the times, the means whereby 'culture' and 'society' could be harmoniously brought together. It was therefore 'English' that was considered by the school inspector Arnold and his followers the 'appropriate discipline for working-class education . . . to be *the* great means for the creation of social cohesion and for the dissemination of an outlook which favoured the unity of classes in matters of ethics and human progress.' [53] 'English', as the study of literature, became interchangeable with the insular, moral order of 'Englishness'.

As Perry Anderson indicated more than twenty years ago, it had largely been the canons of this native literary tradition that occupied a post, at least until the late 1940s, that elsewhere in Europe had usually been addressed by philosophy, Marxism and sociology.[54] It perhaps hardly needs pointing out that this profoundly moral sense of 'tradition' and 'community', deeply indebted to Arnold, to the Leavises and to the institution of 'English', has, in fact, also become a key term in contemporary debates on British culture. It provides the ground upon which cultural identities are assumed to be constructed.

Meanwhile, in the 1950s . . .

The central importance of the concepts of 'tradition' and 'community' bring us back to the work of Richard Hoggart and Raymond Williams, and to the implications of the above discussion for contemporary native cultural analysis and criticism. Both Hoggart and Williams were initially indebted to the protocols of the 'close' and attentive reading recommended by the Leavises. And both were equally interested in illustrating a tradition: that of the working class in the case of Hoggart, that of the 'culture and society' debate in the case of Williams. However, when these authors began extending a 'close' reading 'for tone' to a wider range of 'texts' than that normally admissible to the canons of 'English', the subsequent sense of 'culture' was destined to be amplified and irreversibly modified.

The willingness finally to acknowledge a native popular culture, previously excluded from the realms of good taste, was largely forced upon British intellectuals by the increasing and apparently irresistible presence in contemporary British life of a mass, urban culture, much of it apparently American derived: from the popular press and comics to cinema and dance music. It was not so much good will as an urgent sense of threat that had initially prompted intellectuals involved with *Scrutiny* and then, in a more extensive and generous manner, Hoggart and Williams, to consider taking contemporary popular culture seriously.

This extension turned out to be crucial. But the moral imperative nevertheless remained deeply ingrained. So, jazz and football could certainly be considered, because they were part of two 'great traditions': one, Afro-American, the other of the British working class; but the American detective story, not to speak of the invasion of a very un-British, Hollywood-derived, gum-chewing, gangster-styled, fin-tailed, Lucky-Striked, Coca-Cola-ed, rock'n'rolled, post-war American mass culture, continued to be despised. Here is Raymond Williams in 1961 making the distinction between 'good' and 'bad' popular culture:

> Can we agree, perhaps, before passing to the more difficult questions, that football is indeed a wonderful game, that jazz is a real musical form and that gardening and homemaking are indeed important? Can we also agree, though, that the horror-film, the rape-novel, the Sunday strip-paper and the latest Tin-Pan drool are not exactly in the same world, and that the nice magazine romance, the manly adventure story (straight to the point of the jaw) and the pretty, clever television advertisement are not in it either?[55]

Well, can we? And when Richard Hoggart refers to the culture of the 'traditional' working class we are sometimes offered an apparently Platonic category of a subaltern 'Englishness' that appears as timeless as the stilted moral version proposed by Waugh, or, in a more rigorous language, by the Leavises. This appeal to the values of a native 'culture', to a tradition that is ultimately untouched by the immediate sense of time, calls for a suspended state of disbelief. In the mystique of 'values' it is conveniently forgotten that culture itself is a dynamic construction, that it involves both processes and the continual making, extending and remaking of social and historical textures and connections. Further, such historical processes, which Hoggart, for example, at times certainly recognizes, do not involve a fall from grace, a movement from the 'good' to the 'bad'; in other words, culture does not necessarily involve a moral discourse at all.

What Hoggart presented as a relatively stable reality, albeit under threat, was itself once a novel form of urban and commercial culture that had taken the place of older, more artisan, locally-based, home- and work-based, working-class patterns of life. When he came to write his book in the 1950s this situation was, in turn, being transformed by further developments. But inside that process no one moment – the working-class culture of the 1860s that was replaced by the extensive urban one of the 1890s, or that of the 1920s that was being radically remade in the 1950s – is necessarily more 'authentic', or 'better' than another.

Something of this sense of change and complexity was undoubtedly recognized by the native school of Marxist historiography that emerged in post-war Britain, and which initially culminated in the foundation of the journal *Past and Present* in 1952.[56] The research and writings of A. L. Morton, Christopher Hill, Rodney Hilton, Eric Hobsbawm and E. P. Thompson, and the historical work that emerged in their wake, did much to draw attention to the dynamic and specificity of native popular cultures, customs and traditions. In many ways, it was the development and extension of this indigenous Marxist historiography, and its subsequent application to the pioneering cultural analyses of Hoggart and Williams, that has provided a more cogent sense of the formation of contemporary British culture. In consciously taking up the earlier radical liberal inheritance in the historical work of Tawney, the Hammonds and the Webbs, it simultaneously affirmed and extended the profoundly national axis in historical research with its focus on the alternative, but fundamentally male and public, narrative of the 'free-born Englishman'.[57] It represents what Bill Schwarz calls the 'anglicization of the Marxist tradition, demonstrating its compatibility with a native idiom of critical social theory'.[58]

From Hereward the Wake through Wat Tyler and the Peasants' Revolt of 1381 to the Puritan Revolution, Captain Swing and the people's war in 1940, the Marxist historians sought to offer the unbroken narrative of democratic populism. However, this rather romantic and parochial version of 'Englishness', where all was continuity, lost its tempo after 1945. For if yesterday's worlds presented the uninterrupted evidence of popular struggle and the continual extension of the people's rights and liberties, the 1950s marked the first real moment of stasis and recession in almost a thousand years. But, then, the lack of evidence of native popular radicalism after 1950 could be put down to the invasion of American mass culture and its successful colonization of native tastes; certainly many intellectuals of the day believed that to be the case. In the case of the Marxist historians a declared anti-capitalism served to more rigorously underline the by now traditional native intellectual refusal of industry, urbanization and modernity. The result was that there was little to be said for the present, except its rejection.[59] As Schwarz notes, it was the past, the radical traditions of the 'English', just as it had been with *Scrutiny*, or Hoggart's evocations of working-class childhood, that was decisively set against the present.[60] However, to rescue that past for the present, to equate the 'nation' with the 'people' and the 'people' with a radical moralism, suggests a rather forced dislocation and unwinding of very different histories and contexts in order to achieve a single, heroic narrative of the peculiarly English route to socialist redemption. The historians may well have successfully challenged the literary domination of the question of 'English', but the moral economy that lay behind that domination, including much of its ethnic and gendered assumptions, was not only unchallenged but even amplified in their appropriation.[61] We may well have lost the world of the 'organic community' and radical populism but we have gained a quite particular history – both in the narratological sense of story and the Nietzschean one of fabulation – in its place.

Gramsci goes to Hollywood

Let us look at this idea of a popular, native tradition from another angle. While in the 1930s and 1940s individual British films often encountered substantial success, the wider attempt at creating a 'national cinema' was spectacularly unsuccessful in contesting the overwhelming presence of American films. Successful British actors and actresses in post-war Britain, for example James Mason, Greer Garson, David Niven, Stewart Granger and Jean Simmons invariably went to Hollywood to continue their careers, as did Alfred Hitchcock – frustrated by the limits of the British film industry.

It is also often argued that the Ealing comedies of the late 1940s and early 1950s, by concentrating on everyday popular culture and characters, offered an important contrast to the middle- and upper-class heroes and mores of British cinema and official versions of 'Englishness'. Viewing them today I am tempted to suggest that what they largely offered was a popular view of 'Britishness': the other side of the consensus, the subaltern world and values of the street community, the pub, the Coronation cup, fading sepia photographs on the parlour mantelpiece, the virtues of working and sticking together. It could be argued that this jocular and soft-edged version of lower-and working-class living represented a paternalistic and largely uncontested reproduction of the existing sense of Britain and its 'people'.

In this sense, American films of the period – whether it is the gangster or the private eye film set in the naked city, images of independent women taking control of their lives, the symbolic violence of the Western, the surrealist fantasy of the musical, or the fear generated by the novelty and uncertainty over modern technology in science fiction films, or just simply individuals taking their chances in the modern world – offered far more daring visions. The willingness of such films, particularly in the 1940s and 1950s, to deal with the more complex and problematic world of crime, corruption, passions and violence suggests that their popularity also had something to do with them being more adequate vehicles for contemporary emotions and expression than the insular universe of British cinema. They promised a more 'open' world which was simultaneously richer and more 'real', for in it you can certainly be defeated, be destroyed, and discover that modern life is indeed corrupt, but you can simultaneously discover yourself to be less oppressed and restricted by your immediate culture and circumstances.

That 'America' became a favourite metaphor among British intellectuals for all that was wrong in the modern world clearly had much to do with the primacy of the United States in the world economy, and a subsequent sense of bitterness on the part of British commentators in registering this particular loss of native power. But the real change lay elsewhere, although it was hardly appreciated at the time. It was the dramatically altered reality of cultural production itself in the epoch of mechanical (soon to become electronic) reproduction that was destined, through photography, recorded music, cinema and television, to set the terms for a common language that would constitute what today can be considered as a revolution in perception, æsthetics, meaning and culture.[62]

Against the then prevalent idea of the unilateral growth of a monoculture under the homogenizing impact of the mass media we can today recognize how earlier forms, identities and languages return in different fragments, memories and traces to take up residence in the discontinuous present and there open it up to further possibilities. In this manner, uncertain and ambiguous dialogues with locally-placed but increasingly globally connected futures are kept open, leading to a corresponding shift in cultural emphasis and sense. It was the American economy that initially dominated this transformation, but inside a set of languages provided by the mass media and increasingly experienced in 'our common inheritance – where the wide world impinges whether you wish it or not', other traces, accents and dialects would find voice and the opportunity to transmit it across this shared network.[63]

What would eventually lead to the extensive remaking of the very sense and possibilities of 'culture' was, however, largely obscured in the native rush to defend local 'traditions' from 'Americanization', foreign invasion and alien change. In this conservationist mood, where it was intellectuals who defined and prescribed what was 'right' for the 'people', there can be discerned both the confident Arnoldian sense of cultural authority and, in its parochialism, a profound refusal of modernism which ultimately ignored its wider and democratic potential. With this I do not want to suggest that the post-war popular culture of the United States was inherently more democratic, but, against the narrow traditions and austere institutions of British life, it certainly represented a more extensive and imaginative sense of the possible.

There were, of course, changes going on inside British culture in this period. Internal dissent was manifest in the new realism of the 'angry young men' and their rebellious 'kitchen sink dramas', together with a spate of working-class novels and their transformation into film: *The Loneliness of the Long Distance Runner; Saturday Night and Sunday Morning; Billy Liar; This Sporting Life.* But this 'new realism', and its gritty language of native, male revolt, only offered, in its often misogynist rebellion against domesticity, the other, sullen and subaltern, side of a tradition, rarely a way of breaking its mould. While it proposed a series of decidedly un-showbiz faces in Albert Finney, Tom Courtney and Richard Harris, the possibility of radically different cultural perspectives and possibilities continued to come from outside Britain.

Here we could compare two films: *The Wild One*, an

American film on Californian motorbike gangs starring Marlon Brando that was released in 1953 but initially banned in Britain, and the local version of male rebellion, *Saturday Night and Sunday Morning* that appeared eight years later. The latter is an evocative rendition of working-class life, rebellion and culture, steeped in Hoggartian detail. Its pace, handling of character, language and narrative devices, constitute a 'good film'. *The Wild One*, by contrast, is thin, its acting almost hammy, the story virtually non-existent, the drama predictable. Yet if *Saturday Night and Sunday Morning* with its careful recreation of time, place and custom is a 'good film', *The Wild One* belongs to the world of myth: like the motorbike riders who come and go to 'nowhere', it has the power to symbolize everywhere, an *atopia*, a contemporary opening and chance. While *Saturday Night and Sunday Morning* is a text whose richness and detail confirms a native way of life, *The Wild One* suggests another, largely unknown, one.

This is a sharp verdict, and the story, with all of its particular pleasures and possibilities, of course, does not conclude here. To justify it we perhaps need to remind ourselves, given the prominent role it has played in recent British Marxism and cultural analyses, of the link between cultural hegemony and common sense developed more than half a century ago ago by the Italian Marxist Antonio Gramsci in his *Quaderni del Carcere*.[64] Of particular relevance here are Gramsci's notes on 'popular literature' and 'Americanism and Fordism'. In both he castigates native intellectuals for failing to establish a dialogue with the popular mass culture of the day. In the second set of notes he identifies in the 'intellectual' and 'moral' resistance to 'Americanism' the defensive refusal of a 'possible new order' represented by the emerging forms of American industrial production and its mass culture. Untroubled by 'tradition', 'Americanism' threatened to sweep away the passive and sedimented character of European 'tradition' and 'civilization'.

For Gramsci, the question was not so much whether there existed in America a new civilization or culture that was now invading Europe, but that the weight of the American economy and its methods of production were destined to shift 'the antiquated social-economic axes' of the old world and transform the material bases of European culture. Sooner or later, and pretty soon in Gramsci's own estimate, this would lead 'to the forced birth of a new civilization'. It is therefore perhaps worth while underlining that the oft-quoted Gramscian concept of the 'national-popular', and its project for a radical and political sense of culture did not exclude commercial or American inspired forms.

To this remarkably open reading of 'Americanization' there is to be added the well-known Gramscian elaboration of 'hegemony'. With the concept of *egemonia* the simple idea of the direct ideological domination and manipulation of subaltern social forces by a ruling class is replaced with the proposition that ideological domination – the everyday acceptance of the world and its existing relations of power and social relations – is not imposed from 'above', but established across the shifting fields of relations that constitute a shared 'consensus'. This consensus has to be continually constructed and produced inside the different fields of public representation and social life; it involves not merely political but also 'intellectual and moral leadership'. In other words, the exercise of power becomes a decentred and profoundly cultural affair. In the wide ranging and continual struggle over 'making sense' as, for example, in cinema, the hegemonic view seeks to install itself as the consensual vision, as what is 'right', as the perspective that most makes sense. It seeks to be accepted as 'common sense'. Clearly a regard for 'tradition', which is, above all, a cultural construction, where what is 'right' and 'makes sense' is preserved in historical memory and identified with the fate of the community, with a social group or class, and, ultimately with the nation, has much to do with the formation of a native 'common sense' and a historical cultural bloc.

In Gramsci's elaboration we can perhaps appreciate how, even in their languages of dissent, popular forms that look to tradition for their 'authority over perceptions of reality' can unconsciously participate in the complex reproduction of a cultural conservatism, the status quo and a particular hegemony.[65] It is in such contexts, that 'foreign' influences, as Gramsci himself pointed out, can provide a radical alternative.[66] In Britain by the 1950s, 'America' and all it seemingly stood for – consumerism, modernism, youth, the 'new', the refusal of tradition – could, and did, represent a more significant challenge to a native cultural hegemony than more local forms of opposition based on more traditional affiliations.

Petrol pump æsthetics and changing identities

The two small boys who sat behind me were only interested in filling stations. 'Oo, there's a petrol shop', they cried every time. 'I'n't it pretty?' They are lucky, those lads, for if their taste does not improve, they will be able to travel on all the main roads of England in an ecstasy of æsthetic appreciation.

J. B. Priestley[67]

There is a scene in the film *True Stories* (1986), immediately after the song 'Wild, Wild Life' has been played in a club, where the camera pans the forecourt of a night-lit filling station in slow motion. This shot, which encourages us to dwell on the unexpected beauty of common place objects and situations, is not only a possible reply to Priestley's incredulity but also recalls the æsthetic ploy of Pop Art. Completed around the same time as the film is the Lloyd's building in central London; Richard Roger's peculiar amalgam of architectural high modernism – smooth surfaces, steel, glass, functional – and pop: symbolic, spectacular, image conscious, against the grain. The æsthetic and cultural re-evaluation of the common place in fact owes much to Pop Art and the subsequent recognition of the novel cultural importance of post-war popular culture and what its detractors generally referred to as 'Americanization'. These collective tendencies affected what Benjamin aptly defined as a 'tremendous shattering of tradition', and have led to the eventual relocation of the native literary canon and its 'culture and society' tradition within a far wider set of concerns in which teddy boys or women's magazines could become as significant as T. S. Eliot.[68]

This particular story of the remaking of post-war taste and culture is by now extensively documented.[69] What perhaps can be added is the simple observation that the formation of what we today understand as British culture is still being defined. The suggestive alternative and 'otherness' that was once stated through the 'foreign' manifestations of modernism, and subsequently concentrated and brought home in the diverse emphases of Pop Art, subcultural styles, pop music, 'Americanization', and then in the recognition of gendered realities, race and ethnicity, for example, has opened up the earlier and more narrow mode of 'Englishness' and spilt its complex heritage over the present world. It points in particular to the previous exclusions from the discussion, where the inarticulate were not granted a history because, according to E. J. Hobsbawm, they 'were not its makers but its victims'.[70] Listening to these diverse voices and experiences, tracing out their histories and their contribution to an ensuing complexity, the existing syntax of native representation – of which criticism and critical thought is one of the languages – is surely forced to adopt a less assured key. As a minimum it should suggest a different axis in cultural analysis, where the fundamental opposition in British cultural debate is perhaps no longer to be perceived as being 'between culture and anarchy but between tradition and democracy'.[71]

This latter line of enquiry leads inevitably to a significant decentring of previous sense, explanation and history, drawing into the discussion elements that are both internal *and* external to that shadowy but persistent point of reference which is the nation.[72] The presence of the once unrecognized, of other worlds and points of view, inaugurates the decentring process and opens up an incessant interrogation. It is in this particular opening that the limits of the inherited 'culture and society' tradition become most marked.

The ties that bind

fiction seeps quietly and continuously into reality, creating that remarkable confidence of community in anonymity which is the hallmark of modern nations.

Benedict Anderson[73]

No single tradition can function as a guarantee of the present, can save us. There are many, constituted by gender, ethnicity, sexuality, race, class, that criss-cross the patterns of our lives. By bringing them into history, into recognition and representation, we appreciate the complexity that can challenge the tyranny on the present of a single, official heritage: that of 'being British'. At this point, tradition, historical memory, 'roots', become important less for themselves, as though tokens of a vanished 'authenticity', and more as suggestive, active signs, stimulating a personal and collective confidence in assembling effective passages through the possibilities of the present.[74] In the subsequent commotion, the institutional sense of politics, of centre and margin, of economy and culture, of the 'nation' itself, is necessarily forced into movement and change.

There is ultimately the need to acknowledge the limits of the national framework, to recognize that local realities and details also simultaneously participate in other networks, that of black metropolitan cultures, of EEC legislation, or of the international division of labour and the transnational exigencies of capital, for example. It means to recognize that the 'nation' as a heterogeneous cultural and linguistic unit is not a closed history, something that has already been achieved, but is an open framework, continually in the making. In starker terms, it means to move out of the mythological tempo of 'tradition' into the more fragmented and open discontinuities of histories.

The present world does not automatically augur an info-tech paradise of reduced flexi-time work, computer-integrated manufacturing, whirring disks, bleeping monitors and computer printouts (presented simultaneously as the new driving sector of the economy, of modern life and of leisure). It does, however, usher in a new horizon of possibilities. It produces a space (in both the physical, temporal and symbolic sense) in which previous social relations, economic organization and established knowledge and expertise are thrown into question, crisis and movement; in which work may become discontinuous; in which ecology will not be of peripheral concern to the economy but part of the same social budget; in which the gender of power and politics can no longer be assumed or ignored; in which the exhaustion of the post-war consensus and the hardening of certain ideological discourses may, paradoxically, encourage the creation of transversal connections over previous political divisions, as, for example, in the case of sexual rights and freedoms; in which native perspectives may be frequently interrupted and forced to accommodate transnational tendencies and realities; and in which consumerism is not a by-product of industrial production but a self-generating economy and way of life no longer limited to the 'family unit' but now characterized by highly fluid and heterogeneous channels of consumption that, in turn, are symptoms of important changes in the very conception of 'production' and 'markets'.[75] In this *uprooting* and *rerouting* of earlier histories, structures and traditions, in their mutation and contamination in a contingent world, we can begin to discern a wider sense. The combination of such features is forcibly changing the context and nature of existing social and cultural powers, and firmly 'puts on the agenda the emancipation of politics from its subordination to economics'.[76]

The potential sense of all this – which most urgently requires a new sense of both 'politics' and 'democracy', if they are not to disappear forever behind policed poverty, structural unemployment, the legal surveillance and public ostracism of minorities, authoritarian government and into dust-free data banks – has to be discovered and contested in the space of what is potentially and socially possible, and not in abstract solicitations to an absolute 'emancipation', or nostalgic appeals to an imaginary past. For ultimately it is only by testing our imagination on the possibilities of this present – 'the only times we've got', as the painter David Hockney recently put it – that we can hope to reconstruct both in the realization of a 'socialized individuality' (Henri Lefebvre), and attempt to enter another history.

It is with this perspective that we can perhaps begin to cut up and rearrange the elements of tradition, including those of resistance and opposition. For these too, as Gramsci's analysis of political equilibrium and consensus implies, have often been fundamental to the successful reproduction of hegemony. Without them the past would present us with an uninterrupted story of tyranny, absolutism and totalitarianism. Without opposition and subaltern voices, there can be no hegemony. So, the forms in which opposition and minority causes are articulated can turn out to be an integral and crucial part of the successful reproduction of hegemony. For example, much of the recent story of the Labour Party, of the representations of the British working class, and such initiatives by radical intellectuals as *Charter 88*, reflect a common refusal to cut, or at least sufficiently slacken and more openly question, the knot that continues to bind these forces to the same referents – that of 'Britishness', of tradition, of the national mode and mood – that have successfully hegemonized British politics and public accounting for so long.

The solutions that oppositional forces have usually offered

have characteristically been drawn from the same lexicon, even the same emotional stock pile, the same national history book, as the rhetoric and representations so gainfully employed by Mrs Thatcher and her governments in recent years. In fact, the Thatcherite 'revolution' provides a sharp illustration of such a native solution. Its central

> idea of the free market, with its stress on the sovereignty of the individual consumer, was diametrically opposed to all that Toryism previously stood for. To the Tory it was obvious that economic forces should be made to accommodate themselves to the established patterns of social relationships.[77]

However brutal and crude, the Thatcherite revival of the Hobbesian sense of 'possessive individualism' subject to the laws of the 'market', while representing a real break with the previous Tory tradition, actually takes us back to another, even older one. In a paradoxical return to the native sources of liberal theory its contemporary radical edge derives from the fact that 'Toryism' as a cultural formation has come to represent the actual consensus across the political spectrum of much of Britain's political and cultural leadership throughout the twentieth century. Part of the effect of Mrs Thatcher's 'revolution' is to publicly undo this established consensus. The centrality of such a deeply pragmatic philosophy to variants of 'Britishness' today, and hence its potential for popular appeals, hardly needs emphasizing. Its tradition includes not only Hobbes and Mrs Thatcher, but also the Levellers and Mr Tony Benn.[78]

The unwillingness to refuse this repertoire, or at least subject it to scepticism and crack it apart by extending its terms and shifting its grounds of legitimation, for example in and through an increasingly insistent European contextualization, is a characteristic expression of a deeply 'English' sense of opposition. So much, including a lot of radical criticism, cultural analysis and historiography, continues to be steeped in the sense of a national (or at least 'English') tradition. It is as though the solutions can only be sought there; that it lies within us, in an alternative version of the 'national' character, to find a more equitable response to modern ills. To compare local prospects with foreign ones is generally scorned. A national hermeneutics is preferred in which, in the shadow of the long, uninterrupted line that descends from Magna Carta, we 'play out our old roles to the end.'[79] To dig into that particular past in the hope of re-emerging with another, more democratic, more open, sense of 'Englishness' is an honourable task. The problem is that today its terms of reference seem too narrow, its appeal too exclusive. The very idea of the 'English' (and the ethnic, even racial, overtones should not be under-estimated) has perhaps been hegemonic for too long for any hope that it can be successfully remade solely from within. Centuries of presumptuous empiricism, Godliness, mercantile power and Empire may have planted too deep a root. It now needs to be reappropriated within a wider context (and not merely European), where the discourses of democracy and differences must necessarily run freer in order to accommodate other worlds, other vocabularies, other memories.

This does not mean to supersede or simply overthrow the inheritance of empiricism, the historicisms of radical populism and the 'national popular', or the moral imperatives of English literary and cultural criticism. It is not possible to deliberately abandon such an inheritance, to cancel it as though it were a page that can now be torn out of the history book. One is forced to come to terms with such a heritage, to revisit it, to live in its ruins and there in the gaps, openings and fragments to grasp a wider sense of the possible. To set limits to this particular native narrative does not foreclose the further unwinding of its characteristic concerns: translated across a wider dialogue into other languages they will continue to exist as memories, traces, interrogations. To draw a line is to indicate a distinction between an interior, a here, and an elsewhere . . . and therefore the eventual possibility of crossing that line.

Chapter 3

Some metropolitan tales

To investigate the city is therefore a way of examining the enigmas of the world and our existence.

Lea Vergine[1]

Method of this work: literary montage. I have nothing to say. Only to show. I will not draw upon anything precious or appropriate expressions full of spiritual values. On the contrary, rags and rubbish, but not in order to produce an inventory, rather in order to render them justice in the only way possible: by using them.

Walter Benjamin[2]

Aron said, pointing to his glass: 'you see, my dear fellow, if you are a phenomenologist, you can talk about this cocktail and make philosophy of it!' Sartre turned pale with emotion at this. Here was just the thing he had been looking to achieve for years.

Simone de Beauvoir[3]

When I walk through the corridors of the subway, I find that I am assailed by a multitude of signs which, taken as a whole, make up the mythology of the world I live in, something like the collective unconscious of society; that is to say, at one and the same time the image it wishes to give out of itself; and the mirror of the troubles which haunt it. . . . Shown up in the light of day as stereotypes, these images cease to function as snares from the moment they are taken up by a living discourse, which remains the only space for my freedom. I know now that this city which oppressed me is imaginary; and in refusing to submit in alienation to its constraints, its fears, its ghosts I wish on the contrary to reinvest them with my own imagination.

Alain Robbe-Grillet[4]

the proper struggle of people in a state of dispossession to gain their inheritance might be seen not as sordid and mindless greed for the things of the market place, but attempts to alter the world that has produced in them states of unfulfilled desire.

Carolyn Steedman[5]

The City is an ideogram: the Text continues.

Roland Barthes[6]

In Naples, where I live, there are a series of familiar metropolitan signs: a giant 'ghetto blaster' or 'boogie box' painted on the street wall with the phrase 'South Bronx' sprayed above it in 'Day-Glo' in front of which young males break dance every Sunday morning; the interior of a cantina covered in pictures of Bruce Springsteen while a boy shows me a photo of the American singer, which he carries in his pocket as though it were an ID card, saying 'The Boss'; a subterranean passage-way, connecting one of the principal *piazze* to the platform of the underground, completely covered by a graffiti mural – subway art. Naples just like New York, if you want. In other words, like many another metropolitan reality of the day, involved in the wider world through the common languages of cinema, music, television, advertising and the metropolitan styles that the presence of these media disseminate in our everyday lives. But, like any other reality, also full of traces of older, indigenous elements and residual tastes; the felt remnants and echoes of more local accents and histories.

It is in this context that seemingly universal languages, dramas and narratives are each day transformed into local instances of sense:

In every country the media pose the problem of the shifting boundaries between national and foreign, otherness and sameness, repetition and difference. Italian television shows sharply how different cultures mingle and blend on the national screen in a flow of fictions. . . . Further it highlights how *Dallas* is naturalized in popular Naples, how Californian-ness can become part of the imaginary of a Southern Italian housewife, how the proximity of a poor Roman *borgata* to a petty bourgeois household in Rio, to a mansion in Denver, Colorado, is made acceptable and plausible by its appearing on the same flat screen in the same household in close succession.[7]

In the late twentieth century, cities in North America and Europe are coming less and less to represent the culmination of local and territorial cultures. Many of these cities themselves threaten to become residual; abandoned and obsolete monuments to an earlier epoch. Or else, as twilight regions of once confident and rational projects, they are transformed into æstheticized cityscapes (in architecture and art galleries, cultural and heritage centres, loft living and designer homes), while their previous populations, if they have no role to play in this act, are inserted into other discourses: ethnic communities, urban poverty, inner-city decay, industrial decline, drugs, organized crime.[8] This particular metro-network does not simply represent an extension of the previous urban culture of the mercantile and industrial city and its form of nation state; for it no longer necessarily represents a fixed point or unique referent. While the earlier city was a discrete geographical, economic, political and social unit, easily identified in its clear-cut separation from rural space, the contemporary western metropolis tends towards drawing that 'elsewhere' into its own symbolic zone. The countryside and suburbia, linked up via the telephone, the TV, the video, the computer terminal, and other branches of the mass media, are increasingly the dispersed loci of a commonly shared and shaped world. Towns and cities are themselves increasingly transformed into points of intersection, stations, junctions, in an extensive metropolitan network whose economic and cultural rhythms, together with their flexible sense of centre, are no longer even necessarily derived from Europe or North America.

With this semiotic extension in details, and a simultaneous loss in focus, references to an 'outside' increasingly fall away. At the most there is the sweeping urban fringe of endless suburbs, satellite towns and ribbon development, or else inner-city housing projects, unofficial, subterranean economies and those pockets of hard, local, realities – whether Brixton, south London, the back streets of Naples or the *barrios* of east Los Angeles – that are invariably distinguished by poverty, often ethnicity, and local languages of identity. But the earlier separation between an obvious 'natural' exterior and an 'artificial' urban interior weakens and tends towards collapse. The referents that once firmly separated the city from the countryside, the artificial from the 'natural', are now indiscriminately reproduced as potential signs and horizons within a common topography.[9] It is this habitat, the metropolis, as much an imaginary reality as a real place, that has become a myth of our times.

Yet, precisely because of its allegorical extension, we can no longer hope to map the modern metropolis, for that implies that we know its extremes, its borders, confines, limits. We now know that the city we inhabit, the streets we walk in and drive through, has been invaded by an infectious presence. It is no longer the actual city but an image of it that has taken over. Literature, cinema, television, video and advertising have accustomed us to environments that are no longer geometrically organized by streets, buildings, parks, boulevards and squares. The media, and the images of the metropolis they offer, provide us with a city that is immaterial and transparent: a cinematic city, a telematic hyper-space, the site of the modern imaginary.

The metropolis no longer orders space but time. The physical ambient is traversed, sliced and cut up, by individuals circulating and maintaining contact via the tepid heat of semi-conductors, cathode ray tubes, tape heads, answering machines, pick-ups. We plug in, our hands press the buttons, touch the keys, and our distracted bodies close the circuits. Here sense is connected to speed: messages are threatened by instant obsolescence and meaning becomes movement. In this apparently rootless and boundless landscape, where the signifier refuses to slow down and be classified, we experience the semiotic blur and limitless cross-referencing of the ever-present and ever-ambiguous sign. This semiotic vista furnishes a language that, through clothes, styles, fashion, magazines, advertising, music, film, video, television and telecommunications, provides much of the architecture of our daily lives and yet is without apparent purpose. It is a language that exists beyond the obvious sense or isolated 'reading' of the individual sign; it involves a syntax that apparently carries its referents within itself.

The metropolis has invariably functioned as the privileged figure of modernity. Between Georg Simmel's *The Philosophy of Money* (1903) and Walter Benjamin's work on the Paris of Baudelaire in the late 1930s there is, as Massimo Cacciari points out, all of the European 'avant-garde' and the modern sense of 'crisis'.[10] Here the metropolis represents the highest form assumed by both economic and æsthetic forces. The metropolis becomes both a model of economic and social development, and a metaphor of modernity, a metaphysical reality.[11] It provides the (con)text for the 'objective spirit' (Hegel) of the times and its 'nervous intellect' (Simmel). This spirit, the *Geist*, is here revealed in a 'flat materialism' on the surface of things, in the transitory and the contingent, in the instantaneous reality of the modern street, composed of fragmentary signs and a time 'without memory'.[12] (Perhaps it is not accidental that in the moment that it is threatened by metropolitan movement and fragmentation it becomes necessary to reinvent memory, to establish its pertinence by way of a discipline – psychoanalysis – and thereby to grasp it on the threshold of oblivion.)

For Simmel, as for Benjamin, it was no longer necessary to undertake the Hegelian task of revealing the deep structures and their effects in order to appreciate the mechanisms of modern society. It was the urban fragment, and the immediacy of the languages of tactile perception, that they considered to be the 'exemplary instance of modernity'.[13] So, it was the sphere of commodity circulation, for Simmel money itself being the most 'striking symbol of the completely dynamic character of the world', for Benjamin and Kracauer the refuse and scraps collected from the edges of a bourgeois order, that set the terms of their analysis.[14] At first sight, this literature of appearances seems to represent a complete reversal of Marx's earlier analysis which, in the wake of Hegel, had insisted on the distinction between the fleeting form of commodities and their real 'logic' as revealed in the world of production. This had meant giving relatively little importance to the sphere of

circulation and consumption, largely considered as a determined consequence of production.

Marx had sought to establish his analysis of the injustice and
exploitation of capitalism on a rigorous, scientific basis. This
involved him in a double movement that, on the one hand,
drew on the idea of a realm of unalienated 'natural' needs,
and, on the other, looked to the rational justification of
Hegelian logic and dialectical thought, suitably translated into
materialist terms, for the understanding of historical movement
and progress. It is not in ethical terms, but in the philosophical
and epistemological faith that Marx demonstrated in these
languages, that his work can be queried. Marx himself,
however, did foresee in the later development of capital, under
the growing impact of machinery and automation, a subsequent weakening of labour as the measure of social value. The
outcome, and here we return to Simmel and Benjamin, would
be that social relations would be increasingly cut loose from
any referentiality in nature or the physical world of production.[15]

What emerges is an 'artificial' environment that abbreviates
the circulation time of capital by no longer being tied to nature
but rather to its own production as a self-referring value.
Further, the Marxist analysis, while respecting a Hegelian
scheme in which the development of capital moves from the
simple form (the commodity) to the more complex circulation
of what today amounts to transnational capital, credit, interest
and the financial and future commodities markets, does
eventually lead to certain doubts about whether a critique that
operates at the level of the simple productive cycle – where we
encounter the celebrated 'fetishism of commodities' – is still
valid when we arrive at the state of a process in which capital
has now lost all its real referents and obligations to any local or
immediate reality other than its own. In this, like Benjamin's
'phantasmagoric' Paris, or the solipsistic syntax of fashion, it,
too, has become another 'exemplary instance of modernity'.

Nevertheless, the contagious appearances of this global
reality continue to coexist with other elements, traces and
stories; with those hidden areas and economies that although
often un- and under-represented continue to operate beneath
the shadows of the metropolitan image. This other side, this
'other', signalled in discrete, local, gendered, ethnic bodies and

experiences, is also caught up in the same circuits. For if in the contemporary confusion between appearance and reality we encounter the end of 'false' appearances and their hidden, metaphysical 'truth', then there is no longer an alternative representation nor exterior point of view. Tensions and desires remain, but they now exist as differences and distinctions *inside* the network. It is from here, and not elsewhere, that criticism, anger, fear, hope, a sense of injustice, and a desire for freedom and change emerge. This contemporary perspective paradoxically carries us right back to the ancient sense of the metropolis, to the Mediterranean fulcrum of the city as *polis*, and to its centrality in Greek thought in the understanding of justice and social welfare. To the Greeks, to found a city was to seek to establish the discourses of justice, solidarity, freedom and welfare.[16] It is in the present day *metropolis* that these discourses now seek a home.

Velo-city, or more than zero

Paul Virilio, director of the Parisian *Ecole spéciale d'architecture*, has suggested, in what seems a theoretical parody of Futurist aspirations, that the cities of the future will be airports: transit points connecting the movement of millions in flight between one megasuburb and another.[17] That future, of course, has already arrived, and in the most appropriate location: in Texas, midway between Fort Worth and Dallas. The city of J. R. Ewing and amber-glassed skyscrapers designed to withstand tornado winds of 150 miles per hour, opened its international airport in 1978. A year later and it was the third busiest in the world. This back projection of the future is undoubtedly the world of 'postmodernism', where everything is 'larger than life', where the referents are swept up and lost in the signs, where the artificial takes over and Dallas is *Dallas*; where the world is simultaneously signified and simulated.

Enter a modern airport and you can see what inspired Virilio's prophecy. With its shopping malls, restaurants, banks, post offices, phones, bars, video games, television chairs and security guards, it is a miniaturized city. As a simulated metropolis it is inhabited by a community of modern nomads: a collective metaphor of cosmopolitan existence where the pleasure of travel is not only to arrive, but also not to be in any particular place . . . to be simultaneously everywhere. This is a condition experienced not only by the contemporary traveller but also by many a contemporary western intellectual: the *flâneur* becomes a *planeur*.[18]

Immediately after take-off, the world flattens out to become a map. It now becomes possible to draw connections over vast distances, overlooking local obstacles and more 'down-to-earth' objections. Gaining further height, the flight plan only needs to consider the relationship between the plane and the flat referent beneath its fuselage. At this point, the effects of events elsewhere are incapable of penetrating our space. Meaning contracts into the pressurized cabin. Life inside the plane, and the views it affords, become more 'real' than the reality we distantly observe.

Flight: to fly, but also to flee. For there below remain more stubborn referents – persistent, material, even to the point of being geological – that periodically pierce the daily networks of sense: poverty, oppression, discrimination, violence, riots, rebellion, war, famine, earthquakes, volcanoes, radiation, death. Temporarily connected to the media, the adjectives these events generate hang in the air, symptoms of vital connections. Close up, the world acquires alarming details, a startling complexity.

'The whole world *can* be plasticized' (Roland Barthes)

If there is, among all words, one that is inauthentic, then surely it is the word 'authentic'.

Maurice Blanchot[19]

Baudrillard says that nature only exists because there is the city, the 'natural' because there is the 'artificial'. And the imaginary. . . ? , the imaginary where the natural is only a counterpart: emptiness, the negative, the other side of the moon? In the western mind, the natural is the 'heart of darkness', an empty sign, the place of self-destruction for civilized being.

On the beach strange bodies come into indiscrete proximity in a collective exposure to the sun, the sea, the wind, and inquisitive glances. Elsewhere this would be considered 'out of place'. While here, under the sign of 'nature', it is permissible.

Two Germans, naked in front of us, are methodically devoting themselves to a return to nature – washing their hair and clothes in the sea – thereby blocking our more modest aspirations to the 'natural'. Both their simulation of 'nature' . . . and ours . . . are, of course, simultaneously equally 'false' and equally 'real'.

The post-, post-, post-feminist girls stretched out on the sand talk of their lives in every detail – their fucking lives – looking aside every so often to ensure that the others are straining to hear.

The south, the south . . . it is here where the 'raw' experiences of nature are sought. Urban space invaders delight in the under-development, in the subterranean and sub-Mediterranean language of another world. A mule, straining beneath the weight of four gas cylinders, struggles up the path that connects the tiny port to the whitewashed village perched 100 metres above the sea. The whole scene is obviously so much 'closer' to nature, altogether more 'authentic'. (There is the 'threat' of a crane being installed in the near future.) Refreshed by these experiences, the tourists depart with their trophies – their sun tan, their photos, their memories and mementoes – for the 'cooked' environments of their cities.

To sink or swim in the imaginary: the abandoned houses of Piscità, silent, deserted ruins slashed open with their wounds facing the sea. Amongst them, an upturned, red plastic boat on which grass grows. In one of these spaces a German girl hung herself with a belt: seventeen and 'only a tourist'. Death has no sense outside culture. Three days later her body is still waiting to be taken to the main island for an autopsy. The hydrofoil would not take her; 'perhaps the ship will', someone says with a mysterious smile. Here there is a space, a gap, between two worlds. We coolly discuss this in an attempt to exorcise such indifference. On our return we learn that her death had been in the news. She was a friend of Toni Negri's son.

The child's red shoes abandoned on the sea-wall. The more they are photographed, the more elusive they become; like the plastic boat, which was also red.

Piscità, again. These cracks in the houses, these openings on a sea of black, jagged rocks, on a volcanic beach: there is no way of getting to these openings except through the cracks in civilization, the gaps in construction, in finalizations, where a seventeen-year-old German girl – 'a tourist' – arrived.

The bamboo slide down beside us on the beach, on this island covered in bamboo where orange and black striped birds fly; the naked body of a woman with long black hair: two benevolent signs in the bitterness of a confrontation without consolation.[20]

In the chronological movement from the singular novelty of the late nineteenth and early twentieth-century city to the wrap-around reality of contemporary metropolitan life in the western world we cross an important divide. The city and its particular forms and gadgets (arcades, department stores, electricity, telephones, cinema, cars, freeways and skyscrapers) initially stood out against the surrounding world. What it offered could be condemned or else explored via a new æsthetic (Poe, Baudelaire, Benjamin). But in either case the distinction between it and elsewhere remained crucial. It was that distinction which permitted both the criticism and the unforeseen possibilities and pleasure of the urban experience. The city was surrounded by *nature* which represented the site of origins and being, the source of opposition to the artificial and instrumental bodies of technology and subsequent alienation.

The panoramas of advanced capitalist societies have increasingly become metropolitan. Not that we all necessarily live in a city. But we live in a network, or, better still, an electronic topology in which the apparent has been transformed into the immediacy of the transparent, and face-to-face contact supplemented and increasingly displaced by the interface of the screen.[21] In these panoramas – from the nineteenth-century urban spectacle of gigantic canvases of battles and historic events, through photography, cinema, television and the computer screen, to the complete æsthetic invasion of space – we discover visualscapes, soundscapes and imaginaryscapes, together with their technologies and cultures, that provide ways of looking simultaneously into our everyday experiences *and* into 'nature'.[22]

Nature simultaneously appears to us as the authentic site of our being and as a cultural and social construct. In this paradox, increasingly explored and confronted in the inter-

active ecologies of our planet (from the German *ökologie* formed
on the Greek *oîkos* meaning house in the sense of habitat), the
social 'origins' of nature are increasingly brought home in a
series of metropolitan projections subject to our interventions.
On the one hand, the 'otherness' of nature is simulated and
maintained by the travel agency, the holiday, the car trip, the
cinema, the handy-cam video camera, the wild game reserve,
the national park and conservationist legislation ('Save the
whales . . . the ozone . . . the Amazon . . . '). Via these means
we apparently reach into nature in the very moment that we
construct it and bring it into history, into the non-natural
(unnatural, artificial) environment of our lives. Simultaneously,
however, the tendency to reduce nature to an anthropological
reality, to a global garden or world zoo (something that may
well prove necessary for the eventual survival of many of its
species), does not rule out some rude surprises 'waiting in
ambush like the suburbs on the edge of the metropolis, with
their own declarations of reality'.[23] For the social production of
nature through or in difference does not rule out an ultimate
indifference. Although we seek to reduce the universe to our
measure and *our* knowledge, it remains apart from us. It is this
divergence, this separateness, this something else that lies
beyond the present state of our language and knowledge, that
ultimately underpins the human adventure: there exist worlds,
at both micro and cosmic levels that exist independent of our
will, of our being.[24]

Most of us, however, in our everyday lives experience nature
not as an alterity observed through the particular protocols and
theorems that focus the microscope or telescope, but as an
altogether vaguer cultural referent. Here nature is absorbed
and rearticulated in and through the symbols, languages and
histories of culture. It is inside the networks of culture, and the
metropolitan variant in particular, that our experiences and our
sense of reality are constructed, thereby permitting the
paradoxical assertion that, strictly speaking, there no longer
exists neither the natural, nor a separate reality, nor naked
experience.[25] What we receive has already been digested and
regurgitated by the organs of metropolitan life, and is
therefore, with respect to a metaphysics of pure, non-
mediated, presence and being, a *simulacrum*.

Nowadays, the concept of the simulacrum is notoriously

associated in theoretical circles with the name of Jean Baudrillard, and, in a wider and more popular vein, with the science fiction worlds of the late Philip K. Dick. It might, however, also be useful to recall its genealogy by referring to the statement made by the German philosopher Friedrich Nietzsche, that most acid critic of 'reality', that 'with the knowledge of the origins the insignificance of the origins increases'.[26] Nietzsche's drastic re-evaluation of appearances and his insistence on their 'truth', that is on the fundamentally constructed and fabulated character of the world, drew him to elaborate his celebrated idea of the 'eternal return'. For if we live in a world, that is, a world of *our* making, in which there is no ultimate foundation to nature or being, then there can be no 'original', no zero point, or day of creation, from which everything commences. There is only the secular (and social) infinity of reproductions, of copies of copies, of simulacra. Our very being, without guarantees or origin, is qualified by the 'eternal return' of being, which is a parody of origins, a simulation.[27] The 'real' dissolves into the simulacrum, into a mutable, historical construct (rather than the metaphysical form that Baudrillard, for example, seems to attribute to the idea of a simulacrum). It is *this* world, this construction and its languages, histories and heterogeneous complexity, that is our unique habitat, our *only* possibility.

In *Twilight of the Idols*, Nietzsche concluded that the 'real world has ended up becoming a fable', and Walter Benjamin, in his study of nineteenth-century Paris, argued that the world appeared as a phantasmagoria, as a dream: the 'phantasmagoria' of the world of commodities is precisely a world in motion, in flux, in which all values are transitory and relations fleeting and, Benjamin gloomily concludes, indifferent.[28] But this world, this day-dream, is also our home. The point is how, in a perpetual tension between its presence and potential do we make it habitable; how do we make it *our own*? The 'pure' or 'authentic' referent does not actually exist. So, even the choice to wake up from the dream and 'return to nature' is itself a simulacrum, for it is something that is reactively formulated from *inside* the constructed and simulated reality of our habitat. We now find ourselves dealing in possibilities and choices, deliberate constructions and responsibilities. Here the sense of the world cannot be set against the metaphysical idea of 'authenticity' and nature in the abstract, but against tangible options and events that are socially and historically produced and which, therefore, potentially remain *within our grasp*.

The 'inauthentic': our only chance?

Central to the culture of advanced capitalism is the cyclical measure of the commodity: holidays involve a package, music is a product, food, clothing and services involve, or do not involve, value for money, meanwhile factories are designed and the work-place styled. Where the image is triumphant the earlier distinction between use and exchange value is increasingly confused. To separate out such categories appears an increasingly arbitrary act, a metaphysical pedantry whose appeal to the premises of an absolute authenticity and natural order against which to measure 'false needs' and 'consciousness' seems merely to echo dully in the vaults of a dead academicism.

The distinction between use and exchange values was extensively elaborated by Karl Marx over a century ago in his critical analysis of the capitalist mode of production. What is to be noted is how the distinction put forward by Marx in the first chapter of *Capital* between use-value (its utility) and exchange-value (human labour in the abstract as mediated by money) has frequently colluded in subsequent discussions with a Romantic view of 'natural man'. Marx himself was actually altogether more careful in his conception of nature than many of his followers. For Marx, Nature in the abstract did not exist. Nature was a productive force and hence, as for Nietzsche, a social and historical construct that was produced and reproduced by social beings as part of a human geography.[29] He considered it folly to look backwards for a previous, more 'natural' state: 'It is as ridiculous to yearn for a return to that original fullness as it is to believe that with this complete emptiness history has come to a standstill.'[30]

Nevertheless there is a tendency in Marx, as the above quote with its reference to 'fullness' and 'emptiness' hints at, that has subsequently been amplified in European Marxism in projects organized around the 'pathos of authenticity' and declared attempts to recuperate the original use-values hidden beneath present day commodity exchange.[31] The idea of human nature which, after the exile of alienation and the odyssey of (pre-)

history is finally to be fully recovered in a hypothetical future is readily assimilated to the Marxian discourse on value. There is here an important tension, already noted in discussing the ideas of culture and nature, that has left a sustained mark on much of subsequent critical thought. While nature is considered a social product, the idea of use-value invariably appeals to the world of 'natural' needs, which, to put it simply, is abstractly set apart in what can only be considered a pre-social world. So, on the one hand, there is the historically determined social product, on the other, an idealist, often romantic, appeal to an abstract value. Whereas Marx located the realization of that value in the further development of the forces of production leading to the realization of a future communism, most other proposals have been distinctly nostalgic in tone, usually involving attempts to re-appropriate an assumed, non-alienated, reality located in mythologized 'folk' cultures and pre-industrial production and art.[32]

The assumption of 'natural man' and a utilitarian appreciation of 'real needs', has often led to considering consumerism as the irrational and empty sheen of a capitalist manipulation. It can lead to 'a sort of æsthetic necrophilia' which 'has to ransack the past because it has no way of conceiving of the present, or the future'.[33] Both the utilitarian distinction between rational choice and irrational needs, and the romantic one between natural being and inauthentic experience, here subconsciously harden into ideologies of nostalgia and a very mixed company of shadows (William Morris and F. R. Leavis, D. H. Lawrence and Martin Heidegger . . .). This is perhaps where the joking, self-conscious, postmodern playing with the past, and its refusal of the moral note of authenticity, begins to take on wider shape as an alternative statement (particularly in the obsessively backward-looking context of Britain).

In the present world, where the time of apprehension has been reduced to that of a Polaroid, where the folds and depths in 'reality' have been apparently ironed out, and the question of 'values' seemingly whittled away, first by the insistent rhythms of industrialism and now by the pervasive media circuitry of late capitalism, where do we go, what do we do? This possibility was considered by Marx himself over a century ago. Scattered among the pages of the *Grundrisse*, that immense series of notebooks that eventually formed the backbone of *Capital*, there are frequent references to 'the universalizing tendency of capital' which lead to the creation of 'new powers and expanded intercourse on the part of individuals'.[34] The problem, as Marx goes on to point out:

> is that this entire development proceeds in a contradictory manner, and that the working out of the productive forces of wealth, knowledge and intercourse appears in such a way that the working individual alienates himself (*sich entäussert*); relates to the conditions brought out of him by his labour as those not of his own but of an alien wealth and of his own poverty. But this antithetical form is itself fleeting, and produces the real conditions of its own suspension. The result is: the tendentially and potentially general development of the forces of production – of wealth as such – as a basis; likewise, the universality of intercourse, hence the world market as a basis. The basis as a possibility of the universal development of the individual, and the real development of the individuals from this basis as a constant suspension of its barrier, which is recognised as a barrier, not taken for a sacred limit.[35]

It is perhaps worthwhile underlining what Marx is suggesting here. The conditions for a new sense of being in the world, one that is more liberated and potentially richer, commence from the actual world we inhabit. And by 'actual' I mean both the immediacy of local realities and the equal force of global tendencies ('the world market'). It presents us with a complex perspective, even more complex than Marxian analysis might itself initially entertain. For if there is a criticism to be made against Marx it is that he tends to overemphasize the role of the forces of production in determining the future course of events. There is in Marx a not infrequent recourse to what Gregor McLennan calls a 'philosophical teleology of history', in which the tendencies of capitalism, its development and eventual replacement, become 'natural laws'.[36] The history of the future is thus already revealed in the 'rational kernel' of the present day forces of production. There remains the strong philosophical intent in *Capital* that suggests that existing contradictions inevitably seek a harmonious resolution in a higher plane, in a transhistorical truth. In an inverted

Hegelianism, this state of grace – the end of history as we know it – would not be the realization of the *Geist* or world Spirit, but a material, human nature that is finally free from alienation and the fetters of previous modes of production.[37]

The paradox lies in the fact that existing contradictions and tensions have their own particular claims on reality, and they do not inevitably call out for a higher resolution in a rational harmony. In other words,

> it is probably true that we are alienated, divided from ourselves, and expropriated. However, this is not a condition which necessarily contains its opposite: the potential for our liberation. Rather, this is the condition in which we have to operate, and is one which will not necessarily end.[38]

For what is ultimately important here is not the identification of the eventual 'end of history' and our philosophical fate but the recognition and realization of tendencies and possibilities that produce 'not only the alienation of the individual from himself and from others, but also the universality and the comprehensiveness of his relations and his capacities.'[39]

So, although we may choose to refuse the speculative finality of Marx's analysis, an important residue clearly remains. Capitalism involves not only repression but also the announcement of new forms of living and previously inconceivable forms of liberation. It does not and cannot develop freely and autonomously simply according to internal 'laws'. It is continually conditioned by the social and historical relations in which it is embedded. For by capitalism we mean not just the precise logic of its mode of production but also developments occurring elsewhere in the formation of the leisure, culture, home, family and 'free time' of the social individuals that constitute the historical forces of production and which remained completely marginal and purely incidental to Marx's own analysis of nineteenth-century capitalist society. Stripped of a philosophical goal, the techniques, tendencies and analyses of such a society free us from the metaphysical weight of a philosophical mandate for reality: 'reality loses all those characteristics once assigned to it by a "naïve" view of the world (the presence of a foundation, the need to relate to, to address and to conform to it)'.[40]

This does not mean the end of reality; on the contrary, now freed of a prescriptive referent and ontological closure, it leads to its extension and complication. It is finally here that our plastic and seemingly inauthentic world comes finally to be recognized in its *potential* to be moulded, modified, transformed and made to fit our possibilities, hopes, desires, needs. For it is this prosthetic world and its languages that, paradoxically, finally provide the only authenticity we can ever possibly know and experience.

Bodies, histories and hieroglyphs

The body is the inscribed surface of events (traced by language and dissolved by ideas), the locus of a dissociated self (adopting the illusion of a substantial unity), and a mass in perpetual disintegration. Genealogy, as the analysis of provenance, returns us to the articulation of the body and history: it exposes a body invested by history and history ravaging the body.

Michel Foucault[41]

We reach into the past across the detritus of time and return it to the present through such contemporary textures and associations that supply its continuing tangibility. It is like a walk among abandoned warehouses and rotting wharves where we observe the details of a rusting crane or a window fitting. In these cases, it is frequently the most obvious and the banal that provide the richest cyphers. The use of cement in place of stone, of asphalt instead of cobblestones, of plastic instead of wood, are the realized choices of a particular world in which æsthetics and industry, culture and commerce, design and desire, entwine . . . the stones do speak. It is what, in his study of nineteenth-century Paris, Benjamin continually referred to as the relationship between what happened and what flares up in the 'now' (*Jetzt*), the relationship in which images and memories are encountered, that is, in language.

Nowhere is this relationship perhaps clearer than in the unfolding syntax of fashion, where every detail has a story, is a sign. Fashion involves a perpetual wager to avoid mortality. Constantly recycling the past in search of the new, its cyclical logic of return and revival has apparently nothing to do with history as such. A fashion revival, for example, has no intention of rediscovering or faithfully quoting a specific historical moment; rather, it revisits, recycles and re-presents a particular look, a sartorial gesture that has become part of the timeless catwalk of contemporary mythology. Fashion is ultimately an abstract art. Georg Simmel noted in 1895 that fashion eschews the utilitarian laws of practical clothing. In its place it proposes a daring attempt at translating the fragile æsthetics of the novel into a temporary tendency, a style.[42] Hence its fatal fascination: the genesis of fashion ultimately rests on rapid decay and a precocious death.[43]

And yet not only does fashion have a history, it has many.[44] In Britain, one of its more spectacular offshoots – where its predominantly male character has run against the popular grain of both masculine stereotyping and the public association of fashion with female culture – has been that of post-war youth subcultures.[45] Since the early 1950s these particular expressions of a popular male look have provided a wardrobe that has left a profound imprint on the development and nature of the British fashion industry, particularly in the significant commercial and stylistic passage from *haute couture* to 'street credibility'. Over the surfaces of the contemporary commercial scene subcultures have affected what Dick Hebdige once characterized as the 'theology of the look', the world of the conditional tense, the 'as if . . . world' of advertising.[46] It is a world seemingly at one remove from daily routines, where our bodies are cut-up and reassembled in quotations borrowed from the other, the imaginary, side of life.

In one sense, all British subcultures have represented stylistic replies to the question of class; a way of responding to one's social condition at a symbolic level, a stepping outside of time and context. So we could add that they thereby also represented a chosen cultural 'exile' in their conscious and unconscious attempts to go beyond the immediacy of class and community referents. To imitate the slouch of a Hollywood gangster or the pout of his girlfriend was temporarily to extract yourself from the weight of a local past; it was to conquer the limits of your own history and confidently, if only temporarily, manipulate a language, a code of desire and imaginary identification. Subcultures, and youth cultures in general, have gradually separated out their particular imagery from the world of daily labour and its immediate social contexts. Allowed to float free of immediate referents the result has been a kaleidoscope of styles, and an increasingly sophisticated semiology of goods, that, drawn into an endless shopping list and an ever more rapid stylistic turnover, has spun right out of the orbit of a precise subcultural history. What it has left behind is a rich coffer for eventual retro fashions, ironic revisiting, suggestive appropriations and irreverent revivals.

Since the photogenic fashions of teddy boys, mods and rockers – now historicized in dramatically 'realistic' black and white shots: very 1950s and 1960s-ish – other stories have emerged, further spaces, margins and more malleable styles have been revealed. There has been an overlapping, semiotic deviancy and a generic confusion that, culminating in the self-conscious cut-up style of punk, has displaced classical white, male subcultures from the arguments of exclusion, urban romanticism and stylistic contestation. The firm and exclusive referents that once guided the teddy boys or the mods in their distinctive options in clothing and music are apparently no longer available. Their logic has been overstretched, over-exposed, dispersed, appropriated. Only the skinhead – recalling a mythically 'authentic' reality: the hard, masculine world of the proletariat that is mirrored in his boots, braces, shaved head and tattoos – refuses this ironic and facetious relationship to the present and the past. The skin, deadly serious in his aggressive nostalgia for the local traditions, street pride and sense of place of the white working-class community, remains a stubborn referent in an increasingly mobile landscape. He, for although there are skinhead girls the symbolic figure is unambiguously male, proposes the simple, timeless truths and identities: those of the nation, of race, of masculinity, of class.

Elsewhere, there is the sense of a new cultural economy in which everything is a little less precise, a little more complex. Where there are boys *and* girls, black *and* British, youth *and* Asian, hetero- *and* homosexual, leisure *and* work (or unemployment), public *and* domestic cultures, older distinctions begin to collapse and give way to less traditional, multiple, less historicized, hence 'lighter' (not to be confused with less serious) and more open prospects. The allegory of class revealed in youthful style statements in the 1950s and 1960s has been complicated and decentred by the plural co-ordinates of gender, sexuality and ethnicity.[47] In youth and not so youthful cultures it has been collage dressing and musical eclecticism, where, for example, it has been not only the confidently declaimed 'roots' authenticity of contemporary black music (dub, toasting, rap, scratch), but equally their (post)modernist æsthetics of chance construction, deft bricolaging, sonorial archaeology and recycling, that has dominated the 1980s. Where subcultures once offered a 'strong' sense of stylistic opposition to the status quo and the world of 'them', the 'straights' and the 'squares', this has been extended and then gradually reworked into a wider sense of detailed differences; the 'Other' becomes more simply, but no less significantly, the 'others'. Here the Gramscian and Foucauldean concept of power returns to remind us that its organization, and subsequent resistance to its imposition, is rarely encountered in a bloc but rather emerges inside the heterogeneous channels and networks that constitute everyday life.

This complication of social and symbolic power has been accompanied by the formation of a new critical common sense in which feminism, the gay movement, ethnicity and race, and the emergence of new cultural (and consuming) subjects, have become part of a wider daily reality.[48] The boundaries – between styles and sexuality, gender and generation – have become fuzzy. The demarcation is altogether less rigid. In the contemporary languages of representation (photography, fashion, music, critical writing) a strategy of inflection has taken the place of obvious distinction and opposition. It has led to a conscious working *within* the available signs and their possibilities, rather than simply *against* them.[49] All this, as Janice Winship has suggested, is quite central to an understanding of such image-conscious 1980s magazines as *The Face* and *i-D*.[50] Inside sign-saturated worlds and schizophrenic rhetoric, where reality and fantasy merge and become indistinguishable, eventual coherence is left to us. Across a flexible economy of apparently indifferent and amoral representations, where the only message that remains is apparently that of the medium and image itself, the reader is left constructing, modifying, changing, contesting, or refusing, the conditions of sense. In the naked light reflected off the glossy page, the photograph or the screen, ethical and political responsibility, no longer delegated to the institutional reproduction of moral platitudes, perhaps finally comes down to us, becomes *our* choice, *our* responsibility.[51]

Representations, languages, stories . . . The realities of race, gender, class, sexuality and ethnicity are not only increasingly represented (in both the æsthetic and political sense), but socially conditioned and constituted, through the 'artificial' languages, the hieroglyphs, of commodities and their accompanying symbology. Clearly, not everyone, for both economic and cultural reasons, has equal access to this circulation. Those who have not, usually minority groups and cultures, or to whom it is forbidden (women and girls in fundamentalist households, for example), often remain excluded, hidden on the other, invariably domestic, side, of *this* particular history and its particular range of cultural possibilities. Representations are not necessarily representative.[52]

But the acknowledgement of such limits, and thus eventually of the further realities that lie beyond this preliminary boundary, is initially drawn out by the public inhabitation of such signs. Playing with the signs of gender, of race, of sex, of ethnicity in print, music, image and lifestyles has constituted an important recognition (and subsequent extension) of social and cultural protagonists over the last twenty years. Here, although so far in Britain they have had only a muted and sometimes thwarted impact on the more traditional institutions of power, the realities of feminism and sexual politics, black identity and culture, ethnicity and race, pollution and ecology, have dramatically increased the pressure on expanding the existing limits of political representation, and with them the very definition of the 'political'.

Where many of these signs emerge and are organized is across and through our bodies. It is our bodies – dressed, undressed, disguised, accentuated, in movement, in pose – that not only provide a ready map, a body map, on which to observe how the different histories of society, fashion, sexuality and race traverse and compose a surface in common, but which in turn are moulded and transformed by such an investment. To watch a video clip, to observe the rapidly changing sartorial regimes that orbit around the sounds and fashions of pop culture, and to open the pages of such an indispensable guide to their movement as *The Face*, is to be presented with the actual physique of some of these possibilities. The body, however focused, distorted, or stretched out in song, sound and fashionable pose it may be, appears as the unique referent among the vertiginous accumulation of designer labels, dance floor sounds, Swatch watches, Perrier water, and other fashionable attachments. Here the body represents the physical locus of the permanent 'yes' of being in the face of the doomed activity of fashion (eternally destined to die in order to keep its discourse alive).

But body imagery not only involves a symbolic game with fashion and mortality. If the male sex continues to represent the abstract measure of the world, the universal 'he' of mankind, then physical attributes are themselves a complexly coded text, script and language directly inscribed on our limbs and skin. We are not all men, and neither are we all white. It is from such distinctions, such differences, that specific moments of power, culture and politics also emerge. It is the body, as individual history, memory and trace, which sets in play the possibility of dialoguing with our being-in-difference. Here a surplus of specificity, an excess of details and sense, points towards the impossibility of erasing difference, where difference functions not simply as a rhetorical or stylistic trope but, above all, as a historical experience.[53]

Central to this highly visible and visualized culture is the construction and presentation of 'woman', the use in particular of her corporeal presence as a means of organizing meanings in contemporary society. Through advertising, through the sale of images, lifestyles and attitudes, women are frequently represented in a chauvinistic, sexist and racist fashion: to be a woman is to be an available woman, open to the voyeuristic gaze, object of the look. $he, to employ Richard Hamilton's visual metaphor, represents the most extreme case of cultural and commercial exploitation.[54] Yet the public world of advertising also depends, as Judith Williamson points out, on the creation of differences and a subsequent realization of distinguishable images.[55] This can be put down simply to the fact that it must encourage you to buy type x rather than type y of what is essentially the same product. It does not follow, however, that advertising simply involves a single system of semiotic (or commercial) differences; it can also encompass more extensive symbolic investments. From the combination of female consumerism, of choices of make-up, of clothes, of music, of domestic appliances, of fashion, of foodstuffs, of furniture, emerge diverse bricolages, personalized or customized images, a set of fragments transformed into an enframing of sense that connect in different ways to the present. In this wider perspective a space opens up for a certain ironic distance, a self-knowing appropriation, a certain willingness to play with these different signs and to decide how to play and where to stop. Perhaps, it is less the content of advertising and its reference to the closed logic of commerce ('Buy Me!'), and more the evolving possibilities of its language and the access it can provide to the wider dialogue of potential, of change, in which images can be chosen, adopted, adapted, inhabited and cast off like a set of clothes, like yesterday's fashion, that is finally more significant.

For women in particular their public image has invariably been associated with their bodies. Under the impact of feminism, that particular inheritance has been both refused and then self-consciously exaggerated, explored, cut up and rearranged.[56] It has often resulted in a contemporary montage of the 'female' whose self-managed flexibility and mobility has uncovered the possibility of short-circuiting the inherited 'look', turning it into an icon of ironic disturbance, not necessarily the object of the male gaze but an unsettling mime of female appearances.[57] Here we could return to the world of advertising, add female images in fashion and film, and then consider the following passage by Luce Irigaray:

> To play with mimesis is thus, for woman, to try to recover the place of her exploitation by discourse, without allowing herself simply to be reduced to it. It means to resubmit herself – in as much as she is on the side of the 'perceptible', of 'matter' – to 'ideas', in particular to ideas about herself, that are elaborated in/by masculine logic, but so as to make 'visible', by an effect of playful repetition, what was supposed to remain invisible: the cover-up of a possible operation of the feminine in language. It also means to 'unveil' the fact that, if women are such good mimics, it is because they are not simply reabsorbed into this function.[58]

Commenting on this passage, Mary Russo has suggestively drawn out the 'critical and hopeful power' of such mimesis and masquerade: 'Deliberately assumed and foregrounded, femininity as mask, for a man, is a take-it-or-leave-it proposition; for a woman, a similar flaunting of the feminine is a take-it-and-leave-it possibility. To put on femininity with a vengeance suggests the power of taking it off.'[59] This is to not to suggest that today we are simply witnessing the smooth unrolling of such a history. Here, as elsewhere, we are talking about the possible, about desire, about the shifting tides of historical opportunity and promise, about a sea of events, about local victories and defeats, about a struggling into realization.

There are also other corporeal-cultural distinctions. There is the colour of one's skin. In Britain 'black' has invariably represented the 'other': a loaded metaphor of both refused recognition and the sought-after difference embodied in the sounds and styles of Afro-American, Afro-Caribbean and Afro-Hispanic urban cultures. It has offered a hidden, stylistic referent – 'the cool world is an iceberg, mostly underwater' – for male generations of Britain's own 'white negroes' (beatniks, mods, skinheads, clubland soul boys) and their 'economic raids on the frontiers of the square world'.[60] But since the 1960s black culture has also been transferred from an imaginary American metropolis to becoming a permanent part of British urban life. The once stylistic investigation of the black other is now brought home to become part of the wider yet simultaneously localized and more imperative question of ethnicity – for *both* black and white.

From the signs of 'rude boys' and reggae rebels to inner-city riots, British rap and break-dance crews, black culture, once consigned to the after hours of public life, increasingly insists on its own specificity, its own presence. Earlier responses to the cold currents of British culture and racial discrimination had often involved a necessary, self-survival, withdrawal into Caribbean memories and customs, or, among a younger generation, the establishment of a more militant autonomy that displayed the stigmata of an enforced exile in 'Babylon' through the Rastafarian lexicon of locks, I-tal food, ganja and reggae. Racism, urban marginalization and the threat of semi-permanent unemployment have caused sections of black youth to abandon self-imposed obscurity for a persistent and sometimes angry presence, voicing the fact that they have no intention of going anywhere, whether back to Jamaica or on to

Ethiopia. Rastafarian and Pan-African sentiments have consequently been distilled and refined into the modern black urban styles of 'ragamuffin' culture, and the more pragmatic patterns of being both black and British.

Today, many young black Britons of both sexes sport fashionable Italian track suits and, remixing the examples of New York B-Boys (and Girls) with Jamaican roots, reggae rhythms with rap anthems, dub with scratch, electronic grammar with British syntax, have transformed the multi-ethnic traditions of a once colonial and colonized subject into local and more immediate sense. It suggests a black integration, not so much with the white mainstream as with the wider possibilities of present day metropolitan culture.[61] Diverse *roots* are now displaced and transformed into particular *routes* through the present. Smiley Culture, from Clapham, south London, is a 'lyrics designer' who has provided one vinyl example of this translation between being British and being black ('Cockney Translation'; another cut in the same key is Sergion and Herbtree's 'EastEndah'). In the clubs, among the toasters, MC-ers, dubbers and master-mixers, there are many others.[62]

Once again, this use of the instances of style, of music, of collective images has been initially restricted to overtly public spaces and associated male theatrics. But while black British 'posses' have been joined in their break-dancing by Asian males, young black women have also taken to MC-ing, toasting, rap and sound systems (Ranking Ann, Silhouette, Ladies' Choice). Meanwhile, the cross-fertilization of Indian pop with Western rock music ('Bangra music, a combination of Punjabi folk, Bombay film music and a small dash of disco') has begun to bring a largely hidden constituency of British-Asian girls out on to some of Britain's dance floors.[63] Here the 'community' does not so much bridge East and West as undermine this stark, mythologized, opposition, relocating the differences intrinsic to both Oriental and Occidental cultures in another context, another possibility.

What all this actually means, whether it is merely the discovery of further markets responding to previously unacknowledged needs or the public establishment of previously ignored cultural identities that were hidden in more isolated traditions and communities, or, and this is perhaps where the vital fascination of the question lies, *both*, no doubt is still all being worked out. Perhaps such antitheses are themselves false formulations for a more ambiguous and subtle flux? What is clear is that the mix, in both the musical and more extensive cultural sense, has been extended; that the horizon of the possible and its network of connections has been irreversibly widened, opened up. As Jazzie B of London's Soul II Soul optimistically sums it up:

> What I'm doing is a sign of the times. My generation of West Indian origin is the last of its kind, my children will be almost totally English. We are now living in a multi-racial society. All these mixed people are interbreeding, living together. These things are evident, right in front of our faces, we can see them every day. The Funki Dreds realise this, we understand this, it's the dawning of a new era. Black and white grew up together, we're compatible. People of our age are leading the way and it's important to show that, yeah, we're going to give this a go.[64]

What these particular sets of representations – images of female imagery and mimicry, of black and Asian British cultures – do suggest and begin to make visible, are the norms, the usual discourse of sense and (his)story, in which they are invariably represented and placed. To talk of ethnicity, of black and Asian cultures, of female iconography, fashion and cultures, is usually to talk of certain forms that are positioned, addressed and frequently emarginated by an unacknowledged centre. To challenge that centre, and its tacit authority to speak in the name of the 'others', it may well be mandatory that we, or at least, I, underwrite my 'determined ignorance' of such conditions as being black or a woman.[65] This also implies a decentring of any attempt to explain these presumed 'margins' from what Jane Gaines justly refers to as 'a position of privilege'.[66] This is not to relinquish (my) critical responsibility but rather to recognize limits, boundaries and something that escapes me, while attempting to disentangle or unwrap aspects of these different histories from the discourse that initially positioned, and marginalized, them – that literally attempted to wrap them up.

The emergency is permanent

The tradition of the oppressed teaches us that the 'state of emergency' in which we live is not the exception but the rule. We must attain to a conception of history that is in keeping with this insight.

Walter Benjamin[67]

The freedom that becomes possible in the world of the mass media and an information society is not perhaps the freedom of the emancipated 'subject' imagined by the idealist tradition and, then, in its wake, also by marxism; this 'absolute' subject (totally free, without interior mysteries or limits) was too heavily modelled on God to be realized (it was Sartre, here the inheritor of the idealist tradition, who said that man was the failed project to become God).

This absolute conception of freedom remained totally within the horizon of ideology: it presumed that there was the possibility of an absolute point of view on the world and history, and considered it the task of mankind to appropriate that point of view. But today, now that the information society has demonstrated that the idea of such a total point of view is a myth, the possibilities of freedom and emancipation can finally be redimensionalized and become more human and more 'realistic'.

Gianni Vattimo[68]

Almost twenty years ago the German poet and essayist Hans Magnus Enzensberger characterized the mass media and its 'consciousness industry' as a 'leaky system'.[69] I think it is perhaps useful to extend his verdict to include the whole cultural economy of advanced capitalist societies. I have tried to suggest, in both theoretical asides and through some local indications drawn from contemporary British culture, why the language of exchange-values which constitute this particular view, and hence the 'one-dimensional' reality of its ascribed alienation, is perhaps more complex, open and politically suggestive than is often suspected. We are neither the passive victims of this complexity nor its obvious masters. The 'good' side of contemporary opportunities, despite a pronounced optimism in technological determinism in both Marx's writings and the prophecies of contemporary 'third wave' seers, will not arrive automatically.[70] They may not arrive at all. Precisely because there are no guarantees in a world that has grown dramatically both more complex and more immediate, the need to identify, develop and be involved with such possibilities becomes more pressing than ever.

This leads to a break with earlier beliefs in a homogeneous and unique political or cultural project. As Gianni Vattimo notes, quoting Walter Benjamin's 'Theses on the Philosophy of History', it is only from the point of view of the 'history of the victors that history is a unitary process in which there is consequentiality and rationality.'[71] The defeated and the excluded do not see or feel it like this. It is the winners who write the story, conserving only those parts that can participate in legitimating their power. Even alternative versions, 'history from below', and their accounts of resistance and struggle, often preserve the same consequential rationality in an inverted image: offering the 'lessons' of defeat that will mount up to a final victory. More immediate, discontinuous and irregular sets of experiences, altogether less susceptible to a teleological harmony, are expelled from the account. Lacking the will to recognize a radical heterogeneity can lead merely to the reproduction of existing hegemony through the tacit reproduction of its subaltern voices and oppositions. It is the very authority of history, that story which institutionally seeks to legitimate a continuum of sense, which, as Benjamin insisted, has to be blasted apart. Establishing a dialogue across its diverse, and not necessarily compatible, fragments it becomes possible to establish an exchange that mediates the meaning of our existence.

It has been under the impact of feminism, race and ethnicity, that the abrupt edges of an earlier hegemony, presented in the neutral syntax of knowledge and rational analysis has been most sharply exposed. To reintroduce the uneven and fragmented experiences of the once obscured, hidden and defeated means to reject a homogeneous and unitary sense of culture and politics, of history. Such considerations invariably result in a critical cutting edge in the more usual discussion of the 'political', where cultural details and differences are usually relegated to an instrumental footnote in the discourse. For these other voices are also part of the *polis*. The crisis of politics is precisely the crisis of a discourse that once authorized politics, simultaneously legitimating it and prescribing it, and which admonished those who 'spoke out of place'. The ingression of other voices and histories leads to the preceding sense of politics being displaced. There is no one place which now has the exclusive prerogative on speech. With respect to its traditional sense, politics now confronts an excess of sense. It is this excess that, simultaneously investing distinct realities and histories while maintaining their differences, provides us with the possibility of a shared set of interfaces and involvement, and a political sense of the commonplace.[72]

We come to recognize the existence of 'other worlds', and abandon the presumed security of a unique or privileged point of view. The 'third' world increasingly migrates into the metropolitan centres and discourses of the 'first', and 'woman' appears in those discourses 'as intrinsic to the condition of modernity; indeed, the valorization of the feminine, woman, and her obligatory, that is, historical connotations, as somehow intrinsic to new and necessary modes of thinking, writing, speaking.'[73] The everyday world is seen to be constituted through a mutable framework of heterogeneous differences that are increasingly marked, experienced and understood in a shared or common, network of representations. Here the different histories and details of class, but also of gender, ethnicity, sexuality, race, nation, locality and tradition, are culturally entangled, woven into, and subsequently constituted, by that network. The metaphor of the network, frequently employed in this book, is particularly suggestive; it stands for both a shared context of communications – the common world of the mass media – and for the idea of the cultural labour required (the work) to transform and translate the shared languages that have captured our world (the net of words, images, narratives, and their means of transmission), into a particular sense, space and shape. In other words, it underlines our continual involvement in the active process of networking, in which the net, like any net, is also full of holes, of openings, of possibilities.

The 'truth' – the intellectual, social and political authenticity of the moment – is no longer the object of a theoretical idealism, to be sought beneath the surfaces of appearances, and subsequently set over and against the everyday world, but becomes rather the horizon in front of which we modestly move. The irreducibility of the world to a single, comprehensible, totality, map or source of 'authentic' being, forces us to recognize its incalculable alterity: the differences we need to respect. This, as the philosopher Emmanuel Lévinas has pointed out, undermines the assumptions of the priority of the self and the sovereign 'I' in our understandings and interpretations.[74] Each of us, in our tentative encounters and dialogue with the 'other', have now to face, to face up to, and to look into the face of, that excess which, existing apart from each of us, continues to hold out the promise and possibilities of that charged horizon which illuminates the fragments, memories and languages of our histories, and which in a manner 'human, all too human', we call the 'truth'.

Chapter 4

A handful of sand

In other words, the political question is not to do with error, illusion, alienated consciousness or ideology; it is to do with truth itself. Here lies the importance of Nietzsche.

Michel Foucault[1]

We take a handful of sand from the endless landscape of awareness around us and call that handful of sand the world.[2]

Perhaps we need to try and redefine ourselves in a landscape where it is possible to encounter more extensive, lateral truths.

What for others are deviations are for me the data that define my route.[3]

Therefore to sail . . . across Friedrich Nietzsche's 'open sea':

at last the horizon seems to us again free, even if it is not bright, at last our ships can put out again, no matter what the danger, every daring venture of knowledge is again permitted, the sea, our sea lies there open before us, perhaps there has never been such an 'open sea'.[4]

We live in a world in which the authority of previous guides has apparently crumbled. They have become fragments, bits of a particular archive (of Western Europe, of the white male voice), part of a local history that once involved the presumption (and power) to speak in the name of the 'world'. How we respond to these conditions, what sense we draw from this situation comes increasingly to depend on the recognition that 'it is the *concept of crisis* itself that must be understood *within the idea of truth'*.[5]

The following discussion, drawing upon the figures of postmodernism and Nietzsche, attempts to suggest one possible engagement with that sense of crisis which is intrinsic to thought. It is not offered as a solution or an explanation. Neither postmodernism nor Nietzsche can be said to represent an exit from the contemporary critical condition; on the contrary, they both encourage us to turn back into the present, to sift through the traces, litter and remains of our past, and there extract a wider sense of the possible. For the perspective I wish to suggest is only a possible journey in the face of these questions; a journey undertaken not in order to abandon the present but rather to extend our *dialogue* with it.

The enigma of reason: the æsthetic route

> If an enquiry . . . should fail at last of discovering the truth, it may answer an end perhaps as useful, in discovering to us the weakness of our own understanding. If it does not make us knowing, it may make us modest. If it does not preserve us from error, it may at least from the spirit of error, and may make us cautious of pronouncing with positiveness or with haste, when so much labour may end in so much uncertainty.
>
> Edmund Burke[6]

> these philosophers of the future might rightly, but perhaps also wrongly, be described as attempters. This name itself is in the end only an attempt and, if you will, a temptation.
>
> Friedrich Nietzsche[7]

In order to change things it is necessary to establish a relationship with them. It is here that the recent 'post-modernist' inroad on the rational perspectives and formal concerns of 'modernism' has notoriously arisen. As the Italian philosopher Gianni Carchia has pointed out, at the centre of the æsthetic programme of modernity is the supersession of the earlier connection between art and myth by the critical relationship between art and truth.[8] Within this particular time scale, the 'postmodern' could then be characterized as the passage of that formula into uncertainty, where a secular art proliferates and the formal properties of the 'truth' are altogether less assured.

Behind the noise and spectacle of the contemporary debate lies the extensive working through of the inheritance of the earlier distinctions proposed by Immanuel Kant. The eighteenth-century German philosopher divided up the world of human enquiry into the distinctive spheres of theoretical, æsthetic and moral (or practical) reasoning. In the *Critique of the Judgement of Taste* (1790), which after the *Critique of Pure Reason* (1781) and the *Critique of Practical Reason* (1787) concludes the Kantian trilogy, the judgement of the beautiful is considered to be without finality, to involve a disinterested pleasure. But, although without finality, our sense of beauty is ultimately tied to Newton's 'design of nature' and the 'natural disposition of mankind'. Here it is reason, which functions as the conductor in all our experiences of the incomplete and the partial, that represents, as Kant puts it, 'the totality of a series of generations that stretches towards infinity'. In æsthetic terms this perspective can be threatened by the rupturing instance of the 'sublime' which, unlike the harmonious marriage of the spontaneity of the imagination and the rule of the intellect in the disinterested universality of the 'beautiful', invokes an excess which threatens to annihilate the subject. Nevertheless this threat is eventually contained within the concept of the infinite which is possessed by the subject: it is as if the disrupted relationship between nature and freedom 'redis-covers itself at a higher level and the humiliation of the subject is transformed into the glorification of its superiority and autonomy'.[9]

In Kant's own considerations on taste, and on its limits, there exists an important insistence on the transitory and oscillatory nature of the æsthetic experience.[10] While such an experience appeals to a common, hence universal, sense and sensibility, and eventually to the regulatory principle of reason, it also recognizes the precarious status and 'freedom' of the power of judgement. Now if that uncertainty is extended to the whole Kantian scheme of things, not only our taste, but also our moral judgement and the 'infinity' of critical reason, is put in question. When Nietzsche later attacked the disinterested æsthetics of his predecessor, he wrote:

> Man believes that the world is filled with beauty – he forgets that it is he who has created it. He alone has bestowed beauty upon the world – alas! only a very human, all too human beauty. . . . Man really mirrors himself in things, that which gives him back his own reflection he considers beautiful: the judgement 'beautiful' is his *conceit of his species* . . .
> Nothing is beautiful, only man: on this piece of naïvety rests all æsthetics, it is the first truth of æsthetics.[11]

What is to be noted in the Kantian accommodation of theoretical reason, morality, the question of taste, and their confrontation with the excess and ultimate alterity of the sublime is what this vision briefly entertains and then rapidly occludes. That is, beyond its rational location, and in its sublime apparition, the æsthetic experience can become the privileged site of crisis. For Kant, the sublime marked the limits of reason, its other, ultimately unrepresentable, side. The infinite had to be translated into the finality of thought. But this particular closure invariably opens up a further set of questions. Here, for example, the prudent empiricism of the conservative Edmund Burke leads to a less comprehensible and altogether more radical vision of the sublime; one that is ultimately linked not to our rational limits, but to 'the ideas of *pain, sickness,* and *death*' and the 'strong emotions of horror'.[12] The sublime, for both Burke and Kant, represents the threat of formlessness, the infinite, the unrepresentable, ultimately death. However, Burke's earlier interpretation, with its empirical and physiological reliance on the subjective force of 'terror', 'obscurity' and 'dread', not only lends itself to the Gothic, but inadvertently looks forward, beyond the rational reach of the Kantian system, to the 'raging sickness' of Nietzsche's own 'mortal dialogues' with the infinite. Naturally, Burke himself would have been horrified by the prospect.

Attempts have been made to enter this region of excess, where the apprehension of beauty flees our grasp and tips over into the abyss of fear and a perpetual sense of crisis. Such challenges to the Kantian inheritance and its rational distinction between theory, morality and taste, are to be found in the different proposals advanced in the philosophies of Nietzsche and Heidegger, in Gadamer's hermeneutics, but also, and quite significantly, in Romanticism. They have provided much of the context for the contemporary 'postmodernist' refusal of obvious distinctions between art, philosophy and everyday life.[13] Perceived in this manner postmodernism does not necessarily involve, as its critics usually insist, a deliberately 'kitsch' taste or decadent ontology constructed simply on pastiche and parody, revival and restoration.[14] For if its æsthetic clearly pretends more than a Kantian 'disinterested satisfaction', it is also involved in an attempted movement beyond the Kantian dichotomy of æsthetic and empirical worlds into the wider realms of practical and critical reason. Only this move can sometimes become so radical that all sense of earlier distinction, identification and naming is lost. In fact, the most pertinent criticism of postmodernism is precisely that it is too involved in the wider world, that it is no longer interested in mediation and the labour of representation (whether that involves art or theory), but merely in assembling and collaging already available signs; that is, it does not offer a critical space for the imagination, only an immediate space for the image.[15]

Inside the debate between rational representations and an infinite æstheticism lies an even more urgent contradiction inherited from Kant and the Enlightenment. Here is how Allan Megill in his fine book on Nietzsche, Heidegger, Foucault and Derrida – *Prophets of Extremity* – puts it:

Central to the whole project of Enlightenment thought was the ambition to do for the human world what Newton had done for the natural world. In other words, enlightened philosophers aspired to construct a science of society analogous to Newton's science of nature. At the same time, the philosophers of the Enlightenment also believed in the legitimacy of moral codes. But the existence of a moral code presupposes that people are free to govern their own actions, since entities incapable of governing their own actions cannot be judged in moral terms. There was a radical contradiction between the Enlightenment project for a science of society on the one hand and its continuing belief in morality and freedom on the other.[16]

As Megill indicates, it was Kant's direct dealing with the question of morality (in his *Critique of Practical Reason*) that 'made glaringly obvious the contradictions raised by the Enlightenment project for a science of society'.[17] The eventual response to that contradiction Megill calls 'æstheticism'.[18] Æstheticism, as an attempt to embrace the whole of reality in æsthetic terms, represents a response to 'the Enlightenment pretension to construct a science of society modeled on natural science', and is 'a complaint about the Kantian separation of the practical, the theoretical and the æsthetic'.[19] The æstheticist response is ontogenetic: the world is generated and sustained by language. Following Schopenhauer's insistence on considering the world to be 'my representation', the discourse is then dramatically extended by Nietzsche. 'To put it in the simplest terms: Nietzsche stands as the founder of what becomes the æsthetic metacritique of "truth" wherein "the work of art," or "the text," or "language," is seen as establishing the grounds of truth's possibility.'[20] In this perspective it is already possible to anticipate the eventual æstheticization of the world through the generalization of appearances under the dominion of the simulacrum (language, metaphor, sign).

However, while I personally recognize the imperative that leads to this theorem, in the end I remain unconvinced. Unlike Nietzsche, who, in seeking to break down the walls of the world he has constructed in language, is reduced to scraps of enigmatic speech and eventual madness and silence, or Derrida who provocatively proclaims that there is nothing outside the text, I prefer to inhabit the border country of such discourses. In that intermediate reign of limits it is perhaps still possible to re-articulate such perspectives inside a more realistic (or, more realizable) frame. So, I propose, given a certain scepticism on my part towards the eventual solutions proposed by both the rationalist and the æsthetic proposals, to circle in the margins and to flip between the respective perspectives, both because I believe that there is no obvious exit and because I think that ultimately they are historically and theoretically dependent upon one another. What their meeting does suggest, however, is the possibility of reshuffling the cards in play in order to find another chance, another prospect, in our lives. That, at least, is the temptation.

The desert

if the desert were 'home'; if our instincts were forged in the
desert; to survive the rigours of the desert – then it is easier
to understand why greener pastures pall on us; why
possessions exhaust us, and why Pascal's imaginary man
found his comfortable lodgings a prison.

Bruce Chatwin, *The Songlines*

American cars invariably carry the names of animals or
aggression, and, if possible, a combination of the two: Impala,
Thunderbird, Stingray, Mustang, Firebird, Charger, Corvette.
In Albuquerque I hire a beast, a powder-blue Ford Mustang,
and slipping a cassette into the stereo drive out along the
Interstate into the New Mexico desert.

The desert seduces us with the idea that we can start out
over again, begin from zero: a myth dear to the hygienic
rationality of pure reason and not completely absent from the
demonic æstheticism of Nietzschean thought. But it can also
suggest the idea of the infinite, the infinite language of Jewish
thinking where, unlike the rational finality of Greek *logos*, we
are always dealing with the question of what will be: an infinite
future that conceals its origins, where the inscription of sense
never concludes; for writing 'is not a mirror. To write is to
confront an unknown face.'[21] In the end we recognize that
there is no possibility of going back, of starting over again. All
we can do is confront ourselves and our histories. In the clear
light of the desert, where our actions are overexposed, where,
among the bits and pieces of our existence, time and space
dissolve into one another and the wind blowing up from the
past uncovers patterns in the deposits of our lives, we find
ourselves in a landscape where there is no interpretation
seemingly powerful enough to present itself as the unique
truth. The metaphor of the desert – a privileged topology for
the nomadic sentiments of modern thought – can also become
the place where we get lost, where our existence is swallowed
up and cancelled. For the moment, the only truth on which we
can rely is the immediate contact between the asphalt and the
wheels of our car as we move between towns, motels, TV
screens and billboards, elaborating local 'maps that matter',
travelling down the provisional road we construct between

what has already occurred and the possible . . .[22]

In the past, the French critic Jean Baudrillard, associating the infinity of signs in the contemporary world with the disappearance of sense, spoke of the 'desert of the real' where the signifieds dissolve into the transparency of a perpetual semiosis; what Paul Virilio has called the 'æsthetics of disappearance'.[23] Despite his own hyper-rationalism, according to which the world has become so alienated that it can only manage to be a simulacrum of itself, Baudrillard remains fascinated, intrigued. In *Amérique* (1986) he drives off into the American desert even if this eventually means arriving at the end of a particular intellectual highway. 'We criticize the Americans for not being able to analyze and conceptualize. But these are false processes. It is we who imagine that everything culminates in transcendence, that nothing exists which has not first been conceptualized.'[24]

For the rest of us what does America represent: the laboratory of our immediate future, or the incubator of our nightmares? Perhaps it is neither the one nor the other but more significantly our other, sometimes repressed, sometimes misrecognized, sometimes refused. America offers us life lived in the third person, as myth, as dream, as cinema. To actually go to the United States, and not only to those places privileged in our imagination (New York, Los Angeles, Dallas, California . . .) but anywhere, is to experience the sensation of stepping into an endless film – it lasts as long as your stay there – for everyone talks, walks and lives in houses, offices and cars just like in the cinema. But if our imaginary has been conquered by the hyperrealism of Hollywood the exchange remains complex, open-ended. The pleasure, that *frisson* which accompanies the perpetual movement between images and the imaginary in the montage that *we* put together across the signs and sensations we absorb, brings to the surface that the image, that the fascination with illusion and the æsthetization of the world, that 'America', is also us.

According to Baudrillard, however, the ubiquitous presence of these signs, their consistent invasion of our daily lives, betrays the ultimate exhaustion of meaning. These signs have seduced us, replaced reality with a media-induced reality 'effect', a *simulacrum*, and there abandoned us in a limitless semiotic landscape in which the call for meaning, the possibility of arresting and deciphering the signs, is irreparably lost. The immediate allure of such images screens us from the truth: beyond them there only exists the dead horizon of an infinite nonsense. Modern life has become a desert without co-ordinates, an empty, meaningless region. Signs once referred to something else; they stood in for, and guaranteed, a world of meaning located beyond (or behind) immediate appearances. Now they apparently refer merely to themselves. We are left transfixed, our attention monopolized by flickering screens and neon billboards babbling to each other in the lengthening dusk.

This particular vision, a mixture of exasperated rationalism and European Romanticism gone to seed, casts us into the black hole of semiotic hyperspace where all sense is blinded by the excessive and obscene transparency of a universe choked with signs. But behind this science-fiction scenario I think we can hear the dying echo of the call for a now apparently impossible 'authenticity'. Only now the universe is dumb: no comforting reply is received from space. We are left to wander alone, without direction, in the desert among the semiotic debris of dead meanings. Jean Baudrillard is too sophisticated to suggest that we simply transform this state of affairs into an anthropomorphic galaxy. He remains faithful to his wild rationalism – the universe is thus finally revealed to be alien, ruled over by the meaningless power of The Thing. Like György Lukács and Guy Debord before him, Baudrillard had once grappled with the task of unmasking the alienation of the sign. He recognizes now that it is an impossible mission and succumbs to its fascination. His conclusions, no longer expressed in the Hegelian tones of a philosophical Marxism or the Dadaist language of a Situationist manifesto, but in an exhilarated nihilism, emerge, however, from the same critical language and the same European Romantic tradition, now pushed to the enth degree.

The whole Baudrillardian spectacle is ultimately an instructive diversion, a spectacular playing to death of the generalized motifs of alienation and fetishism. It orchestrates a drama – the obscene simulation of (non)sense – directed by an intellectual discourse that refuses to relinquish its power and let us go. Rather than remaining prisoners of that particular history and its solipsist poetics of a universe that is winding down, it is surely the patchwork explosion of histories around it that seduces us and draws us on.

The critique of the critique

> If philosophy is thought that commences from zero, a thought without foundations, western philosophy is a form of thought that commences from zero in order to arrive at a *primum*. But there exists no passage between zero and one. Nietzsche has unveiled the rules of this game, that is why he is the great *traitor* of western thought.
>
> Roberto Calasso[25]

The contemporary 'return' of the nineteenth-century German philosopher Friedrich Nietzsche indicates a further perspective in what, between critical reason, æsthetics, and contemporary life, is turning into a complex picture. The French Marxist thinker Henri Lefebvre presents him like this: 'With respect to "theoretical man", to classical philosophy, to thought which privileges "pure" knowledge in an authoritarian manner, Nietzsche *decentres* thought. He does not abandon knowledge; he discovers *multiple centres* of knowledge'.[26]

In the opening pages of the *Grundrisse* Marx had carefully distinguished between the 'concrete' and 'a reproduction of the concrete by way of thought'. However, Marx remained a convinced rationalist, for him the 'concrete', although continuing to exist 'outside the head', was ultimately reducible to thought.[27] What was not susceptible to reason could not be epistemologically recognized, could not be theoretically considered to exist. Like Melville's Captain Ahab (and Hegel), he believed that history was fought out between the true and the false, between 'reason' and lies, and therefore that critical work involved the labour of tearing away the mask that hides the true conditions of the world. He never asked himself whether the concept of 'truth' exists; a significant omission 'given that it had been elaborated by philosophers, and given that he placed philosophy among the ideologies'.[28]

As Lefebvre points out, although Hegel and Marx broke from classical philosophy by introducing the concept of difference through their deployment of the dialectic, they both continued to privilege theoretical consciousness and a metaphysics of truth: the domination of nature through thought rather than through desire or needs. For Marx, as for Hegel, theoretical reason defined the essence of 'being'. From this privileging of 'pure' consciousness derives the non-recognition of what it differs from: joy, pleasure, ecstasy, anguish, pain, death.

Nietzsche's reason – *Beyond Good And Evil. Prelude to a Philosophy of the Future* – was 'in all essentials a critique of modernity'.[29] Nietzsche attacked the homogeneous structure of reason that lay behind the nineteenth-century faith in a 'rational' fit between mental structures and the social world as brought about by 'progress'. Such a philosophy, together with its æsthetics, morals and politics, was, he argued, based on the abstract, Platonic metaphysics of western rationalism, where the ideal is considered to be more real, hence truer, than the immediate and the concrete. Nietzsche's proposed move beyond metaphysics represents a break with an abstract theory of being, time, space and identity. He argued that the concrete world had been translated into a mental schema, subject to an intellectual positivism and the uni-dimensional rules of logic . . . 'more useless even than knowledge of the chemical composition of water must be to the sailor in danger of shipwreck'.[30] Such an abstract logic was challenged in the name of the tragic: the immediate world whose insistent presence exposes the fundamental nihilism of a metaphysics, busy constructing a model of sense elsewhere.

Nietzsche's proposal for a more complex intellectuality where reason and consciousness intermix, meant that the philosophical displacement of the body was restored to reasoning: 'if health involves the existence of a "pure subject without will, pain or time" then Nietzsche preferred illness . . . the "pressure of evil": the pressure of the body that has been displaced because it is a source of evil'.[31] This produces a subject who is no longer pure, deprived of will and atemporal, but a 'plural and complex subject, who feels and wants: who is immersed in time and in history. . .'.[32] In the end, of course, Nietzsche is himself only a suggestion, an insinuation of sense, of the possible, not a prophet to be blindly followed or a demon to be angrily expunged; beyond the man, the madman, the jester and the misogynist, lies what until recently has been Nietzsche the forbidden metaphor.[33] His own intemperate language sought to avoid any pretensions to philosophical and political finality, 'everything has become: there are no eternal facts, just as there are no absolute truths. Consequently what is needed from now on is historical philosophizing, and with it the virtues of modesty'.[34]

Marx put Hegelian metaphysics on its feet by insisting that the mental world rests on the material world; Nietzsche went one step further and, subtracting the whole discussion from the teleological context of dialectical thought (which links being to theoretical knowledge, to *logos*), argued that the world in which we are immersed cannot be reduced to the rules of a mental universe.[35] There is no guarantee that our thought *per se* offers us a superior 'truth'. The world – 'everything chained, entwined together' – can only be measured against itself.[36] There is no superior or abstract order, whether we call it God, Nature or Science, to whom we can appeal. In the end, with our traces – metaphors, reason, languages, histories, cultures – we are alone. In this dramatic secularization of knowledge the veil is torn away from the mystery to reveal that . . . there is no mystery, only a complex web of *our* making.

Masks, surfaces and sense

All visible objects, man, are but as pasteboard masks. But in each event – in the living act, the undoubted deed – there, some unknown but still reasoning thing puts forth the mouldings of its features from behind the unreasoning mask. If man will strike, strike through the mask! How can the prisoner reach outside except by thrusting through the wall? To me, the white whale is that wall, shoved near to me. Sometimes I think there's nought beyond. But 'tis enough.

Herman Melville, *Moby Dick*[37]

Surface and depth are not simply metaphors. Three presences – the opaque, the luminous, and their meeting – make up our world; like the past, the actual and the possible. These differences speak to us all, not only to philosophers: the calm abstraction of the heights, the terrible peace of the abyss, the agitation of the surfaces. There on the surface, movement, waves and horizons are delineated. The superficial is freedom. Even if we suppose that in the depths there

exists a monster, Leviathan or Moby Dick, if he never rises to
the surface we could never meet him. The depths hide
themselves, the heights are beyond us. There remains the
surface, infinite and finite. Whatever emerges, whatever
rises from the depths, or descends from the heights, that is
all that counts. . . . Between everything and nothing there is
something.

Henri Lefebvre[38]

So we are caught between the rules of reason and the liberation
of art, between metaphysics and its disappearance, between
representation and its beyond, between the security of the
simulation and the maelstrom of the inchoate. If we look into
the depths we are encouraged to hunt down the whale and
strike through the mask of appearances. Here reality is
mirrored, that is, simulated, and then finally reduced to
thought. Armed with such premises we are encouraged to
gather up the diverse threads of experience attracted by the
prospect of eventually arriving at a 'full' explanation: that of a
Weltanschauung, of a historical 'totality', of the *Geist* or world
spirit. If we choose, instead, to seek a sense in the interrelated
movement of things as they float on the surface we cast a
temporary net, which, like all nets, is full of holes, over a
transitory zone that continues to fluctuate, change and evolve.

Whichever we choose we are forced to acknowledge the
fundamental duplicity of our knowledge. For the construction
of thought is simultaneously marked by a false sense of
coherence and a simulated relationship with an elsewhere that
we call 'reality'. Our knowledge necessarily involves translation, transcription, and mediation, and, with respect to a
metaphysics of 'authentic' being, falsification. Reality is reduced
and represented, precisely in order to permit us the possibility
of assimilating it: thus the character of the simulation – our
concepts, our representations – is necessarily incomplete. In
the play we enact between truth and simulation, we adopt the
latter in order to avoid being overwhelmed and crushed by the
former; we cannot hope to represent the world in its total
connectedness, only fragments, symptoms, suggestions, stories. Thought itself, as Nietzsche pointed out, is a nuanced
fragment amongst the others. And the falsity intrinsic to our
representation is our greatest organic defence, 'without it we

would only be the chaotic movement of the will to truth, which, ultimately, is suicidal'.[39]

It is the self awareness of the life-preserving falsity of thought that lies at the heart of Nietzsche's philosophy. In acknowledging this incompleteness, and setting it against the rationalist repression that seeks to reduce reality to the formal mechanisms of reason, Nietzsche removed himself to the borders of western philosophy, there to dance between regimes of representation following the rhythms of this more extensive 'truth': the truth being that we can never fully know, only act as if we did. The paradoxes and contradictions in his writings are finally unresolvable, irreducible, justly open. They are congruous with the self-conscious simulation of thought, that fragile and immense scaffolding that we cling to and which permits us to continue to act, while simultaneously recognizing the mortal necessity and the foregone limits of our 'act': gesture, simulation, performance, mask, scene. 'We continue to dream, knowing that we dream', *The Gay Science*, aphorism 54. Even more explicit is the following from *Beyond Good and Evil*:

> our fundamental tendency is to assert that the falsest judgements (to which synthetic a priori judgements belong) are the most indispensable to us, that without granting as true the fictions of logic, without measuring reality against the purely invented world of the unconditional and self-identical, without a continual falsification of the world by means of numbers, mankind could not live – that to renounce false judgements would be to renounce life, would be to deny life.[40]

This removal of guarantees and transcendence (religious and intellectual) casts thought directly into the secular world of appearances. The Nietzschean scandal resides in the proposal that the surface is everything, that appearance is being, and that therefore the whole dialectic between 'appearance' and 'reality', between 'surface' and 'depth', so central to the Kantian and Enlightenment tradition, collapses at a stroke. Philosophy which casts away appearances in order to reveal a hidden truth is itself revealed to be a 'human, all too human' illusion; a product of its own conceptual language whose particular resolution it takes to be the 'truth', the realization of the infinite.

To struggle to penetrate the surface, like Hegel, like Marx, and to set the truth against falsehood, is to remain within the philosophical game that Nietzsche sarcastically refuses to play. He refuses to seek the end, the truth, in order to proclaim it and impose it. Values, sense and meanings are not to be justified by some ultimate finality but in the movement of our lives, in their infinite combinations and possibilities (that is, in our finite, our mortal, our unique possibility). We are not directed along the rational tracks of truth towards a future terminus: the end of history and the realization of a non-alienated totality in the reign of absolute knowledge, where in the dialectical unity of nature and history the sense of existence and being become one. We are not necessarily directed anywhere. We are thus finally free to realize the terrible responsibility of our own her- and his-stories.[41]

This suggests a necessary weakening of abstract thought as it dissolves into the languages of a more extensive critical engagement. It declines into a world in which the claims of abstract reason and the search for dialectical identity and the ultimate destiny of history, are pulled up short to be revealed as metaphors. It marks the opening out onto the vista of a more secular, more modest, more fragmentary, and altogether less authoritarian, way of thinking. 'Theoretical man' is finally stricken with the incurable illness and complex urgency of everyday life. In its attempt to reappropriate the world, dialectical thought's exclusive (and excluding) logic becomes itself an accomplice of alienation, its presumed 'totality' (the explanation of the laws of history and forces of society) an unquestioned metaphysics.[42]

To dilute and weaken the metaphysical mode of thinking on critical thought is what the Italian philosopher Gianni Vattimo proposes with 'weak thought' and its 'ontology of decline', where 'decline' indicates the weakening of the autonomous pretensions of reason and its subsequent fall into the world. He has pointed out that the extensive secularization of knowledge that follows such a perspective dramatically under-lines that we live in a world where value emerges only in the transitory moments of exchange. The metaphysics of real and authentic values existing elsewhere, hidden behind alienation, fetishism and 'false consciousness', collapse under the urgent movement of finding, establishing and recognizing ourselves in this world. There are no longer overriding values that control, direct and fully explain the situation, which does not mean that there are no longer values in the world, far from it. There is, on the contrary, a vertiginous liberation of values: 'only where there is no longer the terminal instance of the "interruption", the blockage, of the supreme-value or deity can values find their own nature, that is, through their uninterrupted conversion in a process of continual transformation'.[43]

As has already been suggested, we cannot reach beyond this situation or behind it. There is no possibility of 'going beyond' (the Hegelian and Marxian supersession or *Aufhebung*) our present. There is no guarantee of linear development or 'progress'. We are forced to work with and radicalize what already exists; to return to and rediscover and recover what has already occurred and is in play.

Vattimo's recent discussion of the Lyotard–Habermas dispute raises the objection that Lyotard's declaration of the end of *le grand récit* is itself a *grand récit*.[44] However, Vattimo then goes on to argue that to think 'of the end of the history' is, above all, 'to centre attention on the problem of history as the source of the legitimation of knowledge, and not, on the contrary, to assume that this problem no longer exists'.[45] Here, following Nietzsche's discussion on the Judaic-Christian vision of time, modernism becomes the epoch of a metaphysical-historicist authorization of knowledge, and postmodernism is the explicit querying of this mode of legitimation. In other words, postmodernism is not what simply comes after modernism, or what arises from a completely different set of principles, for it emerges in a critical relationship with the preceding principles: the 'eternal return' around the 'wheel of being'.

This means that the relationship with history and metaphysics is not one of abandon but of resigning oneself to and re-emerging in them, taking them in hand; the approach that Heidegger tried to indicate with the term *Verwindung*.[46] Vattimo continues by suggesting that

the difficulty in the concept of postmodernism revolves around the fact that the end of modernity involves the end of the metaphysical justification of history for its legitimation – the end of the modern forms of metaphysics: that is, of historicism in its enlightened, idealistic, positivistic and marxist forms.[47]

To resolve this question Vattimo proposes the concepts, already hinted at in Nietzsche, and elaborated by Heidegger, of *Andenken* and *Verwindung*. As Heidegger points out, it is the very idea of overcoming or of supersession that constitutes the critical heart of modernity.[48] To try and escape from modernity by superseding it means ultimately to remain within its limits, with its stable sense of foundation and historicism. Given the problematic nature of overcoming, superseding (*Überwindung*), Heidegger proposed to describe the relationship of post-metaphysical thought to metaphysics using the term *Verwindung*. As Vattimo puts it: 'We can define postmodernity as something that has a relationship of *verwindend* to modernity: that accepts it and takes it in hand, that carries its traces as though it were an illness from which we still suffer, that continues with it while at the same time distorting it'.[49]

In this perspective, the 'foundations' of metaphysics are re-elaborated in post-metaphysical thought as events in the history of being, as Foucauldean epistemes, and not as the 'eternal' structures of being and reason. Therefore, being itself is an 'event', a succession of events, that continually recalls mortality and denies the absolute pretensions of metaphysical foundations, without, however, being able to propose an alternative absolute; we are left instead with the 'festival of memory' (Nietzsche). This is the idea behind Heidegger's concept of *Andenken*.

It is an attitude which can also be nominated by the term *pietas*, not so much in the Latin sense where it is concerned with the values of the family, but in the modern sense of compassion and its sense of devotion towards something which, when all is said and done, has only a limited value, but which is important because, although limited, it is the only value we know: *pietas* is the love for life and its traces – those it has left and which come down to us from the past.[50]

It is what Nietzsche, refusing the certitude of 'true' structures, called the 'philosophy of the morning'.[51]

Knowledge, cultural life and social institutions can no longer run to a higher authority. There is nowhere else to go except to the histories out of which they have emerged. Our world, stripped of the possibility of appealing to another source of mastery, simultaneously becomes more lonely and *potentially* more accessible. These are perhaps the 'good tidings' announced by Nietzsche, the beginning of a *'grand politics* on earth'.[52]

A necessary lie?

> Free from what? Zarathustra does not care about that! But your eye should clearly tell me: free *for* what?
> Can you furnish yourself with your own good and evil and hang up your own will above yourself as law? Can you be judge of yourself and avenger of your law?
> It is terrible to be alone with the judge and avenger of one's own law. It is to be like a star thrown forth into empty space and into the icy breath of solitude.
>
> Friedrich Nietzsche[53]

Where, then, does that leave us? Are we now simply adrift in a sea of sensations, subject to the tides of fashion and their momentary fascinations, where the horizon is now so vast and our senses so stretched in the impossible task of encompassing it that meaning (the arresting of sense, the setting of a limit, the drawing of a line) is merely a chimera, a necessary falsehood that permits us the illusion of knowledge . . .?

Prisoners of metaphors are we ensnared in a labyrinth where reason is confused with 'reality', and logic with 'life'; where, to put it in starker terms, representations are tied to repression? This particular genealogy of western thought is, as Nietzsche frequently suggested, perhaps part of a necessary evil: the boundaries that allow a discourse (the 'truth') to acquire a shape and a direction that is able to grasp the movement of the world, to arrest it and cast it into some form of signification. But again, once we recognize that we are dealing in boundaries, limits and organizational theologies, the very status of the discourse, of its claim to represent the 'truth', is forced into a more minor key and an inevitably more sceptical context. It becomes altogether weaker, more modest, as it pushes up against the frontiers of the possible. Touching the limits and recognizing the fragility of our attempts, we finally fall back into the frame of an unsatisfactory social order. And in that recognition we are forced to move once more:

> Whither does this mighty longing draw us, this longing that is worth more to us than any pleasure? Why just in this direction, thither where all the sums of humanity have hitherto *gone down*. Will it perhaps be said of us one day that we too, *steering westward, hoped to reach an India* – but that it was our fate to be wrecked against infinity?[54]

The cassette has now finished (*We live in the city of dreams. We drive on this highway of fire . . .*).[55] Outside the night is falling while our car continues to follow the asphalt snaking across the desert under the first stars of the evening. Meanwhile, the metaphysical totality we think we have abandoned in ruins continues to cast shadows over our journey. Perhaps a sense of totality is an indispensable fiction, a life-preserving lie as Nietzsche would put it, necessary for our sanity, for our continuing movement. But such a prospect, however necessary it may be, can no longer claim to provide access to a transglobal and transhistorical truth. That is why we find ourselves at the end of Enlightenment Highway: not because its concerns (with truth, knowledge, justice, freedom, equality) have dramatically terminated, but because the assumed link between our potential freedom and the Enlightenment's abstract dream of universal illumination (the totalizing pretensions of the *Encyclopedia*) has snapped. Today, in abandoning that highway for other, more modest, roads there lies the final recognition of our responsibilities, where flesh, blood and bone, the hot body of mortality, triumphs over the cold light of an abstract reason.[56]

Out on the border but inside the net

A final distinction between what I am trying to suggest here and the active 'nihilism' of Nietzsche and Heidegger is that both believed that contemporary life and thought was totally alienated, completely compromised by crisis and breakdown.

This idea dominated their thinking. I am not so sure that it dominates mine. And then the concept of crisis, however central it is to our thought, is also a child of historicism. It presupposes a continuity, a linearity, a sense of development that is being threatened. The active 'refusal' of nihilism is the other side of the affirmative reason of modernism. Both remain tied to an absolute, to a metaphysics, that of the historical process itself.[57]

In their very different ways, both Marx and Nietzsche reject the concept of absolute value, but they retain another absolute, 'namely, the historical process itself, in terms of which all particular values were to be understood and judged'.[58] The ultimate difference lies in the reactive and apocalyptic character of Nietzsche's thought as opposed to the underlying teleology and 'progressivism' secreted in Marxist analyses. Whereas for Nietzsche, 'crisis' involved an irretrievable breakdown and exit from the whole western metaphysical tradition, with Marx, on the other hand, crises were the signals of the uneven and overdetermined developments that lead eventually to a further stage in the progression of the social relations of society.

With Heidegger we find yet a further sense of crisis, one that in the end is revealed to be deeply nostalgic. He is obsessed with the question of origins, in particular of words; of recovering their lost meanings and retracing in them a more authentic language of being. In that sense, although they propose very different perspectives, both Nietzsche and Heidegger share common concern with Marx, and all three with the inheritance of Romanticism and the whole reach of 'crisis' induced by capitalism, industrialization, and modern urbanization.[59] In Heidegger's case, the experience of technology, the city and modernity, is certainly not dismissed. But, despite his careful unravelling of 'technology' in its widest sense – as *technē*, and its deeper and ancient connection to the revealing nature of the arts, *poiēsis*, *epistēmē* and knowledge – its modern presence is registered in a suggestively ambiguous but finally reluctant fashion. This emerges in his most direct confrontation with the theme in 'The Question Concerning Technology', written in the early 1950s. While recognizing that it is impossible to refuse contemporary technology and science, Heidegger is determined to test his poetic vision of being – that which issues forth, that continues to emerge, that endures –

against its very cogs, turbines and machinery. So, if technology is the 'constellation' which discloses or reveals the essence of the modern condition, it is ultimately an uncomfortable revelation:

> the revealing that holds sway throughout modern technology does not unfold into a bringing-forth in the sense of *poiēsis*. The revealing that rules in modern technology is a challenging [*Herausfordern*], which puts to nature the unreasonable demand that it supply energy that can be extracted and stored as such. But does this not hold true for the old windmill as well? No. Its sails do indeed turn in the wind; they are left entirely to the wind's blowing. But the windmill does not unlock energy from the air currents in order to store it.[60]

He continues:

> The hydroelectric plant is not built into the Rhine River as was the old wooden bridge that joined bank with bank for hundreds of years. Rather the river is damned up into the power plant. What the river is now, namely, a water power supplier, derives from out of the essence of the power station. In order that we might even remotely consider the monstrousness that reigns here, let us ponder for a moment the contrast that speaks out of two titles, 'The Rhine' as damned up into the *power* works, and 'The Rhine' as uttered out of the *art* work, in Hölderlin's hymn by that name. But it will be replied, the Rhine is still a river in the landscape, is it not? Perhaps. But how? In no other way than as an object on call for inspection by a tour group ordered by the vacation industry.[61]

The possibility that the 'Rhine' had changed, had been complicated by both older and newer meanings accruing to it, that it could simultaneously exist as nature, metaphor, poetic inspiration, power station and tourist attraction, is not considered. For Heidegger is sick for another home (nostalgia: homesickness, Greek *nóstos* return home + *álgos* pain). He is always trying to return there, and for Heidegger 'home' is ultimately situated along the sunlit footpath that leads to the 'clearing in the woods'.[62] The Heideggerean sense of being-in-the-world (*Dasein*), literally being at home, lies back there in the rural mystique, in 'the pagan "moods", in the enrootedness in the earth'.[63] Ultimately, Heidegger's response to modern life was to turn away, to refuse its *unnatural* challenge, and to look elsewhere and seek our destiny in the roots and continuities of western being and thought. Modern technology sets itself upon the world, it does not permit beings and nature to 'be'.[64] Modern agriculture, modern industry, and modern life in general, are seen to carry us away from that possibility.

With Heidegger any intervention, whether it is the Cartesian seizure of being by theoretical consciousness or the modern day food industry, will stand between us and the emergence, the bringing forth, of being. Heidegger's is ultimately a romantic appeal for stasis, a standing still that might allow the past to catch up with, overhaul and reveal the present. We 'late born' remain in debt to the past, to its essence (*Wesen*) as something that persists and dwells in our present. In its ultimate appeal to a 'natural' mode of being-in-the-world – the peasant in the field consigning seeds to the care of nature as opposed to the frozen food factory – Heidegger's version of authenticity goes way back behind both Marx's conception of 'nature' and Nietzsche's productivist view of being and his scathing reproaches to 'natural man'.[65]

In the end, however, even if we join Zarathustra on the mountain top or Heidegger deep in the woods, there is no possibility of a radical exit. No matter how hard we push against the limits we cannot get beyond the ruins of metaphysics and representation. In that direction lies only the babble of madness, or . . . silence.[66] Without signs, representations, it is impossible to think, to conceive, to speak. We seek to embark, to abandon the shoreline for the open sea, but we can never fully get away. We have no choice but to live inside a repetition of a representation without end. We can neither fully attain the immediacy we desire nor completely discard the concepts that simultaneously enchain us and link us together. In refusing the metaphysical solution we fall and decline into the world. The heroic task of reappropriating a lost 'being' (snatched away from us by alienation and fetishism, by modernity) now becomes an altogether less dramatic proposal. It is translated into the more modest but more urgent task of how to 'be'.

Chapter 5

Voices, traces, horizons

I have to some extent, experienced a relationship to a new logos, a logos where one can reintroduce a relationship to the unthought.

Michèle Le Doeuff[1]

There is an intellectual function in us which demands unity, connection and intelligibility from any material, whether of perception or thought, that comes within its grasp; and if, as a result of special circumstances, it is unable to establish a true connection, it does not hesitate to fabricate a false one.

Sigmund Freud[2]

it is possible to believe in writing . . . precisely because, legitimized by 'nothing', it legitimizes the other and ceaselessly begins.

Michel de Certeau[3]

What in the end guards us
Is our being without protection.

Martin Heidegger[4]

Perhaps, after seeking to unravel some of the mysteries of being 'British', wandering in the metropolis, and then almost getting lost in the desert, it is now time to go home. But, then again, it may be that there is no home, no fixed abode waiting for us. There is the sensation of having exited from the old house of language and of now being lost. This is to experience Heidegger's *Unheimlichkeit*, literally 'to-not-be-at-home'. We can never go home, return to the primal scene, to the forgotten moment of our beginnings and 'authenticity', for there is always something else in between. We cannot return to a bygone unity, for we can only know the past, memory, the unconscious, through its effects, that is when it is brought into language and from there embark on an (interminable) analysis. In front of the 'forest of signs' (Baudelaire) we find ourselves always at the crossroads, holding our stories and memories ('secularised reliques', as Benjamin the collector describes them), while scanning the constellation full of tension that lies before us, seeking the language, the style, that will dominate movement and give it a form. Perhaps it is more a question of seeking to be at home here, in the only time and context we have. While 'going home' recalls the nostalgic associations of a mythologized point of origins (our mothers and fathers), 'being at home' in the world involves finding ourselves in a wider, shifting, but more flexible, framework in which our mothers and fathers, bonds and traditions, the myths we know to be myths yet continue to cling to, cherish and dream, exist alongside other stories, other fragments of memory and traces of time . . .

Voices . . .

Innocence has been replaced by the ironic mode, induced by the challenge of complexity; my sense of place and position has given way to the uncertainties of an ex-centred voice. Within that limit I acquire a certain freedom. For although the speaking subject may well now be decentred it is certainly not dismissed. On the contrary, more aware of my limits, I become more self-conscious, more situated, more sensitive to my particular place in a differentiated world. No longer able to speak in the name of the 'others', to assume their voices and experiences and reduce their histories to mine, a previous monologue, spoken in the name of reason, theory, politics or 'mankind' (*sic*) is transformed into the diverse possibilities of dialogue. Cast into the uncertain outcome of this worldly exchange, an assumed intellectual unity – political, cultural, ethnical, patriarchal, Eurocentric – shatters against the complex structures, networks, cultures and societies in which different voices, histories and languages seek connections, sense, hope, a future, an existence.

Literature is today critically received as an incomplete text, full of gaps, limits and silences. Theory and criticism, which, as modes of writing, also constitute a literary genre, are also subject to gaps, limits, silences. We are increasingly drawn to confer meaning on such gaps and silences rather than seek a presumed unity or coherence.[5] Freud pointed out that it is the incomplete nature of analysis that provides the 'only secure interpretation'.[6] What is offered is neither a cure nor a conclusion. It is a critical practice whose activity, condemned to be a part of this world, can reveal elements that are incompatible, even mutually incomprehensible, but whose synchronic presence in the knots of language and experience produce new questions, reproblematize our sense of being and hence reproduce our historical space.

With Freud, reason is extended to acknowledge what was previously excluded. Freud explicitly refers to Nietzsche in his elaboration of a language that alludes to that unknown (*Unbewusste*) which determines our affective, intellectual and social conduct. But, in the movement into the mysterious shadows that accompany our thoughts, actions and ideas, the analysis turns out to be interminable. In the end it proves to lie beyond any clear sense of interpretation, for it cannot unveil the causal and singular instance of the truth. What it offers are temporary conjectures and provisional compromises that can be undone by the discovery of further displacements. There is a continual unravelling of time and fragmenting of linearity through the repetition and displacement of psychic materials. In his 'need to understand the enigmas of the world that surround us', Freud's 'uncanny science' opened up an unresolvable tension, both in his own work and subsequent inheritance, between medicine and philosophy, between psychoanalysis as a cure and psychoanalysis as a critical language.[7] In the attempt to reveal the enigma, the rules of reason were transformed, but the enigma remained.

Beyond these limits we have only 'our illusions of desire' (Freud). We live with them, they are essential, pregnant with the promise of our deliverance, of the Messiah, but they cannot reveal the enigmas of the world. The 'truth' that elides and slips away, that flees our grasp and is always elsewhere (Derrida), deferred to the infinite future proposed in Hebraic times, the enigmatic nature of the 'not yet', the still silent

(Jabès), introduces an ethical relationship to what lies outside and beyond us (Lévinas).[8] The 'small fragments of truth' (Freud), splinters of language and experience, that we hold in custody have no pretence to a mastery but rather represent our responsibility in the dialogue over an uncertain sense.

This opening up of thought in its recognition of the incomplete directs us towards the 'other', towards that presence, that alterity, that reveals an excess that lies beyond a previous regime of knowledge, and which circles back upon the presumed and interrogates its jurisdiction of sense. Such an 'other' is no longer merely the negative pole in the dialectic of European thought and culture. Beyond the immediate plane of metaphor the historical figure of the other challenges the way the world was previously presented and ordered. Once alien categories turn out to involve innumerable bodies and mortal forms of difference: not black people, or the Jews, or women, in the abstract, but real, historical, living individuals who emerge in and from different histories, languages, memories and experiences. To reorganize our thought around these differences can represent a vital attempt to escape from a monolithic and repressive language that has perpetuated so much tyranny and horror, so much fear.

In *L'Imaginaire philosophique* Michèle Le Doeuff says:

> it seems to me that philosophy is not a function of some strictly 'masculine' form of 'rationality', but philosophy often produces a misogynist style of imagination, by trying to be more than it actually is, trying to make rationalisation operate to an extent beyond what it is actually capable of.[9]

This setting of a limit, together with the increasing mobility of the referents to which we appeal, severely questions the operation of seeking to guarantee thought by 'putting it under the "patronage" of an accredited authority'.[10] Such a 'weakening' of thought encourages us to play with how we are 'constructed' and codified by the languages in which we move, negotiate our appearances and to which we necessarily refer for our sense of things; that is, to play – both in a critical and, when possible, joyful manner – with our 'selves'. But that is only the initial move. For we might well hesitate after a moment over applying to this process the adjective 'critical'. Just what does that term mean today now that many of the criteria that once assured its voice – Marxism, class struggle, the 'national popular', or, in other registers: patriarchy, rationalism and science – are themselves subject to criticism and self-doubt; from what space or position does a critical voice speak today? By raising questions about the idealist propensity of theoretical discourse for autogenesis and its unwillingness to live in doubt we are setting a limit, drawing a line, establishing a context. In deliberately weakening the power of its voice and setting it amongst the other voices, the other powers – social, sexual, ethnic, symbolic – that constitute a particular cultural network and its variable place within a wider, ultimately global, reality, we may come to realize that critical responsibility may well lie less in the formal identification, resolution and closure of a question and rather more in keeping such questions open.

The limits of our thought lie not in a refusal or lack of responsibility, but in the recognition and response to the complexity in which both it and everything else moves. In this sense, reason is unable to propose a universal or total vision; it serves rather to undo that request, to demonstrate that it has no possible reply, and to guard us against such proposals.

In philosophical, literary, historical and critical considerations of modernity the figure of woman has invariably been presented as the symbol of all that is mysterious, unknown and uncontrollable: 'The fear in front of woman is the fear before the absence of sense: is the fear in front of the abyss of nothingness that sucks you in'.[11] Such a figure stands for that excess in feeling and being that breaks the bounds of reason and threatens its exercise of power. It is therefore a figure of the displaced, the hidden, the unrecognized. Here it would be possible to delineate another history of modernity, a history that is indicated not only by the public, and predominantly masculine, zone of industrial production, the factory, acts of goverment, and the *flâneur* on the city pavement, but also by the political economy of consumption, by the department store, fashion, dance music, the cinema, soap opera, daytime television and the appropriation of these and other languages in a predominantly female domestic space. While men have sadly annotated the public score of modernity (Benjamin, Adorno, Heidegger, etc.) it has been in the margins, in the displaced matters of women, of ethnic groups, of race, of slavery, that other voices have been heard and the understanding of modernity has been rewritten. In the ambivalent, therefore richly uncertain, whirlpool of metropolitan life, of consumerism, of crisis, other narratives, other languages, and other possibilities have led to that 'fusion of horizons' that constitutes another sense, another imaginary, and a further possibility.[12]

Taking such absences seriously involves more than a simple addition to existing critical discourses. These languages – concerned with the destiny of man in the abstract, that is with non-gendered being – are, in their repressed particularities (white, male and Eurocentric), often even unable to register the question. They cannot face what would decompose their intellectual unity of 'reality'. Their silence becomes the source of criticism and the site of analysis. Examining the place ascribed to women, to ethnic groups and minorities, is to challenge the legitimacy of such discourses to speak in the name of the universal and the autonomy of reason; it represents a challenge to their claims to the truth, to their neutrality, to their pretensions to explain totally.

'Heterosexual men remain unquestioned . . . "Women, blacks and gays". This triumvirate is written and spoken about as though they were distant planets orbiting men's sun.'[13] In his unconscious refusal to consider himself a historical and cultural construction, heterosexual man assumes the form of nature. Perhaps the critical question is not constituted by the presence of women, gays and ethnicity so much as by the specific absence of male heterosexuality?

Traces . . .

Language is what allows access to the open-ended. For language is something that is structured but not foreseeable. In conversing with somebody, with an entity that lies beyond myself, discourse, intercourse and ethics combine in the encounter with alterity, in a responsibility for the dialogue and the difference. It is such a premise, so carefully laid out by Emmanuel Lévinas in *Totality and Infinity*, that distinctly marks the shift from the primacy of sight and its totalizing, that is finite, vision to the infinity of language. For Jabès the infinite – his chosen metaphor is the desert – is the source of subversion: the book that is never complete, that exists beyond the violent closure of *logos* and the limited visibility of theory. In Hebrew the word is not the place of *logos* but the site of movement, of activity. It leads to a relationship with the conditional, where 'the rigid gives way to a diverse language, one which is open and receptive, which is no longer merely logical, but is rather aconceptual and dialogical.'[14] To dialogue with what lies beyond is to acknowledge a desire which is never satisfied, which lies the other side of totality and its regime of sense. It means to occupy a speaking position in which it becomes imperative to listen, for it opens out on to the possibility of a reply. It is a position that at one and the same time inaugurates a refusal of the subjectivism secreted at the heart of an abstract system of thought and proposes an ethics: 'The idea of infinity delivers subjectivity from the judgement of history to declare it ready for judgement at every moment.'[15]

To break with a unilateral sense of history means to abandon a metaphysical purpose mirrored in the passage of time. It means to renounce a knowledge that already knows its scope and to respond to the importance of those uncertain, decentered and ambiguous margins and borders that exist at the edges of time, obscured by the unswerving light of 'progress'. To appreciate this possibility involves taking a holiday from idealist premises, from the ideological critique of reality, from its unveiling of 'false consciousness' and its insistence on the teleological direction of history. Only by suspending these categories in a critical sabbatical is it possible for other discourses, other dialogues, other voices, to be heard.

This tear in the fabric of discourse, and subsequent opening in the languages of legitimation, represents a space in which to relocate and reformulate the questions, problems, struggles and hopes we have inherited. It is where these languages, the histories we inherit and inhabit, the structures and powers we encounter and employ, are further broken down into an extensive complexity. It is a complexity that draws us into the local world of the immediate while simultaneously casting us before a potentially wider horizon of sense.

The question of historiography, the writing of histories and the relocation (and recognition) of past 'events' within present day constructions and concerns, reproposes the infinite space of analysis. Within each context the crumbling landscapes of the past are returned to and reconstructed in metaphor. In writing the past is re-presented, linguistically put together, fabulated, and becomes a narrative, a story, a literary genre.[16] It, too, in the course of events, becomes another historical fragment, a further trace in time. Does that mean that there is no such thing as historical 'truth'? If for history we intend a single and universal container in which all the events, experiences and lives of the past are brought together under the symbol of a unique reason able to explain our sense of being, then our answer would undoubtedly be yes. Such a model of history (and with it, of meaning and politics) has been put in crisis precisely by the emergence of those other stories and other languages previously 'hidden from history'.[17] The Enlightenment and Hegelian idea of history is unable to recuperate these new possibilities for the simple reason that they rarely pretend to resolve the enigma of history; they propose, rather, to commence from that enigma, to explore it, even to immerse themselves in it.

The crisis of Marxism, of certain forms of politics and reasoning, are among the symptoms of the recognition of difference, and, in particular, of sexual and ethnic differences, inside a history in which everything was previously reduced to the same, to a common measure. As Angela Carter caustically lampoons this drive to historical mastery and truth: 'Man lives in historicity; his phallic projectory takes him onwards and upwards – but to where?'[18] If there is no longer the possibility of reducing the differences and complexity of the world to a unique sense, then we find ourselves before a more extensive panorama. So, the idealist aspirations stamped in the house of history are abandoned for a wider landscape and from that perspective rewritten. The pretensions of a historiography, of a his-story, fragment under the multiple impact of other stories. We find ourselves dealing with diverse languages and possibilities whose presence undermines the reassuring metaphysics of a stable reality in which time, sense and identity perfectly coincide. With this I do not want simply to suggest a languid pluralism. For sense here lies not in the separate fates of individualized identities and isolated accounts, but in the interconnected weaving together of the stories, languages, differences and bodies in which we are caught. Sense emerges not in a clear or obvious manner, but ambiguously, from those differences of sex, ethnicity, tongue, time and place, that

propose the unique horizon before which we can construct a
dialogue of meaning.

It is we who take responsibility for the story, for the
particular mix of events, interpretations, tendencies and
possibilities. This is not because we are inventing them, as
though *ex nihilo*, but because the manner and tone in which
they have been 'dubbed' or put together is inevitably a partial
telling, a narrative of exclusion as well as inclusion, an analysis
destined to remain open, to be returned to, rewritten, remixed
and recombined with other narratives, stories and events. By
questioning 'history' and 'truth' we are not denying them; 'it is
rather that they have ceased to be unproblematical issues.'[19]
For if historical reality is not just *there*, neither has it been
wiped out. Between the rational illusion, oscillating between
Hegel's *Geist* and the minutiae of empirical 'facts', and its
ultimate nemesis in a simulacrum, lies the vital network of
voices, traces and horizons in and through which we grasp and
construct our historical, that is, complex and lived, sense of the
world we inhabit.

To reclaim an oppressed past it is necessary first to dissolve
it, to cut it up and free it from the weight of a repressed
inheritance: this is the proposed task of Zarathustra. The past
is recomposed in fragments of memories, voices, and languages, as in psychoanalysis or critical historiography or, more
simply, in the bits and pieces we pick over and put together in
the stories we all construct in conferring sense and elaborating
a poetics of the possible. The oppressive weight of an
accumulative time and reason, and its particular language of
tradition and truth, breaks up. 'While the idea of the continuum
raises all to the ground, discontinuity is the foundation of an
authentic tradition.'[20] Another sense of time, of our time, a
different vision of meaning, another language in which the
repressed and displaced reappear and begin to speak, now
emerges. It is here, producing another sense of the past, and
with it the future, that there lies the possibility of opening a
small 'gate through which the Messiah might enter'.[21]

Perhaps the struggle is not so much for the truth of
knowledge or being, that 'heart of darkness' of epistemology
and ontology, as for the good, for an ethics of living sense
rather than an absolute or abstract knowledge. Is morality to be
equated with reason (Kant) or with life (Nietzsche)?

Horizons . . .

The metropolis is, above all, a myth, a tale, a telling that helps some of us to locate our home in modernity, there to find the new gods, the new myths, called for by Nietzsche. The metropolis is an allegory; in particular it represents the allegory of the crisis of modernity that we have learnt to recognize in the voices of Baudelaire, Benjamin and Kafka. To go beyond these bleak stories of exile and that grey, rainy country of the anguished soul, is to establish a sense of being at home in the city, and to make of tradition a space of transformation rather than the scene of a cheerless destiny. For this metropolis is not simply the final stage of a poignant narrative, of apocalypse and nostalgia, it is also the site of the ruins of previous orders in which diverse histories, languages, memories and traces continually entwine and recombine in the construction of new horizons.

To inhabit a city is to be immersed in a common experience. The expression 'to inhabit' is etymologically connected to habit and its sense of custom and costume (in both the mental and sartorial sense), which, in turn, recalls the Greek *êthos* (usage, character, personal disposition). Further, although *êthos* also refers to the life of animals, to their habits and their nature, to inhabit a city is above all to participate in a significant extension of the term, synthesized in the idea of choice. For we are 'pushed out of the natural order to such an extent that there is no natural ethics able to determine our conduct.'[22] It is the chatter of the city that now maintains this site of discourse and dialogue.[23] In the metropolis it becomes necessary to form new habits and habitats; in other words, it becomes necessary to form a new sense of ethics.

Further, we need an ethics that fully recognizes the body, previously considered as the site of error and evil; that recognizes its languages, written across its surfaces in the alphabets of sexuality, gender and ethnicity; that recognizes its rites and rights, its multiple and differentiated histories. The body is eventually the site of sense. In its desires, details and differentiation it also presents us with a zone of uncertainty; here there are things that flee rational arrest. At the same time, it provides the ground for all those mentioned (and unmentioned) differences that condition the possibility of sense.

There exists a 'reason' of the body, of the unconscious, of the traces of memory, that continually signals something more: the body 'and its great intelligence, which does not say "I" but performs "I"'.[24] This is not to oppose the body to reason, but to indicate a territory which a previous reason was unable to recognize.

In *Berlin Childhood* Walter Benjamin wrote: 'Not knowing your way around a city does not mean much. But to lose yourself in the city, as one gets lost in a forest, that has to be learnt.'[25] That city, the cinematographic and phantasmagoric city with its sensuous streets of desire, is also that imaginary city which has become the modern world. It is a metropolitan hyperspace which acknowledges no exterior.[26] There is no exit, no way out, everything is revealed here in this *topos* of modernity. It is also the place in which we can lose ourselves, experience an absence of direction and belonging. An experience that recalls not only the labyrinthine qualities of city life but also the contemporary experience of art in which the 'beautiful' is not the conciliatory or cathartic property of an object but a contingent experience caught, and then lost, in time and place. In Benjamin's opinion the shock effect sought by Dada is fully realized in the æsthetic turn inaugurated by the cinema and the mechanical reproduction of art in general. Here the 'use-value' of art is fully absorbed and subsequently diffused through the generalization of technical and social exchange. It was, above all, Adorno's continuing allegiance to the sharp, Marxian, distinction between use and exchange value that explains his hostility to Benjamin's seminal proposals in 'The work of art in the age of mechanical reproduction' (1936).[27] In the temporal, hence mortal, space of modern life we discover the constitutive space of contemporary æsthetics; and in the rootless sensation of a loss of bearing and the suggestive and challenging shock of other worlds its constitutive sense.

When the word 'inauthentic' is bandied about we should stop and ask ourselves – 'inauthentic to what?': almost invariably to a presumed metaphysics of being. What, we might ask, learning to live with the critical insights of our mortality, is more 'inauthentic' than that?

It is memory, fear and hope that give form to reason.[28]

In *The Human Condition* Hannah Arendt, perhaps in reply

to the Heideggerean proposal that we are cast into a world whose sense is ultimately constituted by our death, writes: 'even if we must die, we are not born in order to die, but in order to begin.'[29] In reviewing Arendt's book the Italian philosopher Adriana Caverero points out that we are not here dealing with utopia but with *atopia*, that is, not a nowhere but a somewhere, an other place. For the activity of setting out, of commencing, produces an excess that carries us beyond the histories and identities we have already encountered, and removes from under our feet the security on which our sense of history and ourselves has been constructed. It takes us elsewhere.[30]

We dialogue before a horizon of complexities that permits the stories that convince us to take place. It is the conditions of that dialogue, the maintenance of that complexity, that we have custody for. We are responsible for them, there is no one else to guard them. Even Walter Benjamin's majestic angel of history, who contemplated the mounting rubble of the past while being blown irresistibly into the future, is no longer present. There is now only the more modest figure of the angel who has lost his wings and fallen to earth, and a mortal existence, as in Wim Wenders's *Der Himmel über Berlin*.[31]

In Bruce Chatwin's literary landscapes – Patagonia, Prague, the Welsh border, West Africa, Australia – there are traces of voices, histories, events and experiences that unexpectedly interlace: history is undone and recombined. The landscape becomes the laconic scene of dramas lost and then recovered in time, and life 'a cloth woven of stories told'.[32] As a stranger in a strange land the author collects fragments that make up a hybrid world. A sense of bewilderment, wonder and uncertainty reveals a nomadic culture in which we each move with our particular baggage and histories. Traversing territories marked by incertitude, ignorance and the unannounced, 'differences are recognised, exchanged and mixed in identities that break down but are not lost, that connect but remain diverse'.[33]

Other worlds are invariably screened (simultaneously shown and selected) by the world media. The images that emerge frequently resonate with the daily reality of exclusion; further underlined by the 'newsworthiness' of the atypical, the strange, the exceptional. Exclusion is temporarily signalled in

transglobal space. Such representations simultaneously connect and plug into the international media – like the dramatic
demand for democracy by the students in Tiananmen Square
in Beijing and their subsequent massacre by the People's
Army, or the Amazonian Indian symbolically cutting off the
head of a Brazilian government official before the world media
– and yet at the same time continue to signify that they are
coming from a different place, out of another history. It is the
maintenance, even deepening, of these differences that
extends and preserves the horizon of complexity, and with it a
new sense of reality. It suggests an ecological frame in which
the other (as Chinese student, South American Indian, or as
nature) continues to simultaneously exist apart from us and yet
be part of us in a shared responsibility for living in difference,
for being responsible, just as we are for ourselves and the
ethics that sustain such a relationship.[34] This is not simply to
talk of ethical and ecological controls, as though a systemic
readjustment of the logic of development would be a sufficient
correction, but to press for the inscription of these discourses
in our very sense of history, action and responsibility.

According to Wittgenstein the most important part of the
Tractatus was the part not written, the part that lay in the
silence of language.[35] For Edmond Jabès it is the desert, the
silence and the absence of God, that permits the movement of
the word. It proposes a silence destined for voices, just as the
desert is destined for movement. To write, hence to speak and
move, is to break the mould of unicity and become part of an
ethical movement. To speak is to judge.

'Ethics and æsthetics are the same thing' (Wittgenstein,
Tractatus, 6.421).

Writing is not natural. This is its drama. It is an inscription
that tries to come alive, that calls for dialogue. When it
becomes unstable, unsure of its ground, when there is no
longer the illusion that words, sentences and phrases can by
themselves, as though by their mere presence, establish a
design, then language represents a collection of voices and
traces, brought together into a particular mix of which the text
is a record, a testimony. Before the infinity of signs the book
becomes a ship's log, a modest exemplary of the small format
of thought. Writing involves a confrontation with myself and
others. The difficulty of contemplating writing is the difficulty

of thinking the metaphor, of thinking the metamorphosis.

These words, this text, caught up in the wider processes of discourse, of power, is brought face to face with its particular limits; its place in a history, a culture, an ideology, is foregrounded. And when previous boundaries have folded in on the centre; where the 'other' of mass culture and the experiments of the avant-garde no longer represent obvious opposition and alternatives; where the symbolism of yesterday's marginal signs and voices – rock music, subcultures, cultural studies – is now presented as the favourite subject of your local polytechnic and the late night TV slot, then perhaps we can conclude that for many of us our immediate world has been fully commodified and reduced to a common measure. Perhaps, or we could use the occasion to query whether that type of opposition and distinction still holds. Perhaps the old dichotomies, with their reliance on the timeless myths of 'truth', 'authenticity', the 'beautiful', the 'good', and their successive application to æsthetic, political and cultural judgement, have now been transformed into interrogative traces in a more extensive perspective in which elements, stories and relations do not necessarily follow a single logic, do not, as Dana Polan points out, necessarily cohere.[36] When there is nowhere else to go, no theoretical or political enclave that is not inextricably caught up in this world, then we have finally to face up to our direct involvement in the provisional discourses, languages and powers that constitute our present and our presence within it.

To point to limits and inhabit the border country of frontiers and margins robs discourse of a conciliatory conclusion. The domestic scene is supplemented, extended and stretched; and then sometimes overstretched, even subverted. If the precise sense of home and location has been weakened in the spiral of critical dialogue before the infinity of language, metaphor, and interpretation, we have to face up to inscribing (to enrol, to write) ourselves into an altogether less guaranteed context. The inscription of sense occurs before a wider, even incalculable, horizon. This does not mean that the critical voice must abandon the study for the streets, but it does suggest that theorizing, critical reflection and the languages of knowledge, are subject to the questions and doubts that hang over our wider conduct in the world; over what Edward Said has called the 'worldliness' of the text. It is in this more extensive territory that the duplicity of theory with intellectual pretensions to a total or transcendental truth fades in the dusk of an absolutism which has not only violently marked reason, but also innumerable histories and lives. In the 'radical linguistics of thought' the question is conserved as a question; stitched into the folds of time, it opens out onto a philosophical passage that in the end 'is only the widest extension of the concept of history', (Friedrich Nietzsche, *Beyond Good and Evil*).[37]

Notes

The 'double solution'

1 Rosi Braidotti, 'Envy: or with your brains and my looks', in Alice Jardine and Paul Smith (eds), *Men in Feminism* (New York and London: Methuen, 1987), p. 236.
2 Gianni Vattimo, 'Dialettica, differenza, pensiero debole', in Gianni Vattimo and Pier Aldo Rovatti (eds), *Il pensiero debole* (Milan: Feltrinelli, 1983). This is not to suggest that ideology, or dialectical thought, with their metaphysical pretensions to a total reappropriation of the world, can simply be abandoned, as though now superseded, lying back there, behind us, in the past. But there is a sense in which such forms of thinking are 'weakened' and forced to dissolve into more complex solutions and altogether more modest proposals. See Chapter 4.
3 Jacques Derrida, 'Freud and the scene of writing', in *Writing and Difference*, (Chicago: University of Chicago Press 1978); and 'The Purveyor of the Truth', in *Yale French Studies* 52, (1975) now republished as 'Le facteur de la vérité, in *The Postcard. From Socrates to Freud and Beyond* (Chicago and London: University of Chicago Press, 1987). For a useful discussion on Freud and Derrida, see Allan Megill, *Prophets of Extremity* (Berkeley, Los Angeles and London: University of California Press, 1985), pp. 320–32. For further discussion on the role of narrative in psychoanalysis, see Paul Ricœur's *Freud and Philosophy* (New Haven: Yale University Press, 1970).
4 Freud's own description of *Moses and Monotheism*, see de Certeau,'The Freudian Novel: History and Literature', in Michel de Certeau, *Heterologies. Discourse on the Other* (Manchester: Manchester University Press, 1986).
5 Gianni Carchia, 'Pulsione, simbolo, forma', in *La legittimazione dell'arte* (Naples: Guida, 1982), p. 136.
6 Friedrich Hölderlin, 'Note a Sofocle', in *Friedrich Hölderlin sul tragico* (Milan: Feltrinelli, 1989), p. 99.
7 Roberto Calasso, 'Monologo Fatale', postscript to F. Nietzsche, *Ecce Homo* (Milan: Adelphi, 1969), p. 185.

8 Dolf Sternberger, *Panorama del XIX secolo* (Bologna: il Mulino, 1985), p. 28.

9 Luce Irigaray, *Speculum. L'altra donna* (Milan: Feltrinelli, 1977), p. 256; *Speculum of the Other Woman* (Ithaca: Cornell University Press, 1985).

10 Paola Gullì Pugliatti, 'Rappresentare, ri-presentare, tener luogo di: letteratura, storia e altre finzioni', a paper given at the national congress of the *Associazione Italiana di Anglistica*, Bergamo, 24 October 1988. I return to this tension between representation and its limits in Chapter 4.

11 Michel de Certeau, *Heterologies. Discourse on the Other* (Manchester: Manchester University Press, 1986), p. 29.

12 Alain Renaud in a paper given at the conference *Videoculture. Strategie dei linguaggi elettronici*, University of Naples, 23 April 1988.

13 Ludwig Wittgenstein, *Tractatus Logico-Philosophicus*, proposition 5.6.

14 Don DeLillo, *White Noise* (London: Picador, 1986), p. 13.

15 Alessandro Dal Lago, 'Leggi oscure, cose che svaniscono. Note su ermeneutica e scienze umane', *aut aut*, 217–8, gennaio–aprile 1987, p. 233. Dal Lago is quoting Paul Ricœur, 'The model of the text: meaningful action considered as a text', in *Hermeneutics and the Human Sciences* (Cambridge: Cambridge University Press, 1981).

16 A non-linear idea of 'evolution', one which abandons the more deterministic project of 'survival of the fittest' and embraces the shifting and more open complexity that results from the continual co-opting and bricolaging of bits and pieces of inherited structures, can be noted in the writings of such contemporary biologists as François Jacob, Steve Gould and Salvador Luria.

17 See Gianni Vattimo, 'Apologia del Nichilismo', in *La fine della modernità* (Milan: Garzanti, 1985); available in English as *The End of Modernity* (Oxford: Polity Press, 1988). I have borrowed the concept of gendered stories from the Sankofa Black Film and Video Collective video *Territories* (1985).

18 The terms 'hard surfaces' and 'local knowledge' come from Clifford Geertz, *The Interpretation of Culture* (New York: Basic Books, 1973).

19 Roy Bhaskar, *A Realist Theory of Science* (Leeds: Leeds Books, 1975).

20 Roy Bhaskar, *The Possibility of Naturalism* (Brighton: Harvester Press, 1979), p. 27.

21 Gilles Deleuze, *La logique du sens* (Paris: Editions du Minuit, 1969).

22 For example, in Peter Dews's *Logics of Disintegration* (London: Verso, 1987) we find a comprehensive overview of French post-structuralism (Derrida, Foucault, Lacan, Lyotard) presented with an admirable rigour, so typical of much contemporary Anglo-American critical work. Yet, whatever one feels about the particular judgements arrived at, what finally remains untouched are the assumptions of such 'rigour'. In the 'Preface' Dews refers to the tension he himself felt between the 'power and inventiveness of post-structuralist thinking' and 'an awareness that many of its implications ran counter to my most deeply held political

convictions.' He concludes: 'I have tried to work through this tension theoretically, in the belief that the logic of disintegration *can ultimately be resisted on logical grounds'* (p. ix). (My emphasis.) In this appeal to logic as the ultimate court of appeal, apart from noting a singular coincidence with the preferences of native British analytical philosophy in which questions of ethics and metaphysics are often deemed 'meaningless' (A. J. Ayer, *Language, Truth and Logic*, 1936), we might also want to object to what seems a premature shut-down and a false sense of resolution. Whatever the criticisms to be advanced against post-structuralism (or any other anti- or post-logical analysis), aren't 'logical grounds' themselves subject to a certain social, cultural and political scepticism? Isn't a critique carried out on such grounds ultimately an excursus in setting limits, and hence, a *limited* exercise? Or is its particular rationale the unique factor of truth?

For whatever doubts one might hold over the various perspectives unleashed by post-structuralism, one thing it has successfully established against the embedded positivism of the structuralist enterprise is the deeply inventive or *fictive* component of all analytical operations. In the social life of the materials we seek to explore it is the 'logic' of our narratives that attempts to confer sense. Their purpose is to *propose* a complex perspective rather than unilaterally *resolve* it. Whether we consider a particular narrative or analysis satisfying or 'truthful' is ultimately determined by what we feel to be its adequacy in explaining not merely what is logical but also the rich and heterogeneous *texture* of the situation in question. Such an analysis strives to be coherent not to an abstract, intellectual totality but to a social sense of the possible. Given the complex social, cultural and historical cross-indexing involved I remain sceptical that an analytical investigation can be satisfactorily reduced to 'logical grounds'.

23 For more on the Nietzschean 'sea' see Chapter 4.

An island life

1 Quoted in Tom Nairn, *The Break-up of Britain* (London: Verso, 1981), p. 40.

2 In fact, it has been suggested that the Second Reform Act of 1867 'demonstrated that the liberal state was organized to counter mass democracy and universal suffrage', Stuart Hall and Bill Schwarz, 'State and society, 1880–1930', in Mary Langlan and Bill Schwarz (eds), *Crises in the British State 1880–1930* (London: Hutchinson, 1985), p. 12. On the successful organization of a popular Toryism around the images of the 'nation' and the 'people' in the late nineteenth and early twentieth century, see Bill Schwarz, 'Conservatism, nationalism and imperialism', in James Donald and Stuart Hall (eds), *Politics and Ideology* (Milton Keynes: Open University Press, 1986). Finally, the recent shift by both radical and

conservative commentators to consider the concept of 'citizenship'
– see Mrs Thatcher's speech to the Conservative Party Conference,
Brighton, October 1988, Chantal Mouffe's 'The civics lesson', *New
Statesman & Society*, 7 October 1988, Stuart Hall's and David Held's
'Left and rights', *Marxism Today*, June 1989 – suggests that here
there is now indeed the basis to open a new chapter in Britain's
political culture.

3 On history, see Gareth Stedman-Jones, 'The pathology of English
   History', *New Left Review*, no. 46, 1967; on literature, Raymond
   Williams, *Culture and Society* (Harmondsworth: Penguin, 1961).
4 Carolyn Steedman, *Landscape for a Good Woman. A Story of Two Lives*
   (London: Virago, 1986), p. 8.
5 These were: Perry Anderson's 'Origins of the present crisis', *New
   Left Review*, no. 23, 1964, and 'Socialism and pseudo-empiricism',
   New Left Review, no. 35, 1966; and Tom Nairn's 'The British political
   elite', *New Left Review*, no. 23, 1964; 'The English working class',
   New Left Review, no. 24, 1964; 'The anatomy of the Labour Party –
   1', *New Left Review*, no. 27, 1964; 'The anatomy of the Labour Party
   – 2', *New Left Review*, no. 28, 1964.
6 Martin J. Wiener, *English Culture and the Decline of the Industrial
   Spirit, 1850–1980* (Penguin: Harmondsworth, 1985).
7 See Perry Anderson, 'The figures of descent', *New Left Review*,
   no. 161, 1987.
8 This has been thoroughly argued in Geoffrey Ingham's *Capitalism
   Divided? The City and Industry in British Social Development*
   (Macmillan: London, 1984).
9 Gareth Stedman-Jones, 'Working-class culture and working-class
   politics in London, 1870–1900: Notes on the remaking of a working
   class', in B. Waites, T. Bennett and G. Martin (eds), *Popular Culture:
   Past and Present* (Croom Helm: London, 1982).
10 Barbara Taylor, *Eve and the New Jerusalem* (London: Virago, 1983).
11 See J. M. MacKenzie, *Imperialism and Popular Culture* (Manchester:
   Manchester University Press, 1986).
12 The quote comes from Benedict Anderson, *Imagined Communities*
   (Verso: London, 1983), p. 138.
13 Michael H. Levenson, *A Genealogy of Modernism* (Cambridge:
   Cambridge University Press, 1986), p. 15.
14 Quoted in Levenson, ibid, p. 10.
15 ibid, p. 15.
16 Centre for Contemporary Cultural Studies (eds), *The Empire Strikes
   Back* (London: Hutchinson, 1982).
17 Naturally, there have always been exceptions. But, at a general
   level, fundamental change in native intellectual practices in the
   social sciences, for example, occurred only after the invasion of
   'foreign', largely French, theories in the late 1960s.
18 Gayatri Chakravorty Spivak, 'Can the subaltern speak?', in C.
   Nelson and L. Grossberg, *Marxism and the Interpretation of Culture*
   (Urbana and Chicago: University of Illinois Press, 1988; London:
   Macmillan, 1988), p. 271.

19 Homi K. Bhabha, 'The Other question: difference, discrimination and the discourse of colonialism', in F. Barker, P. Hulme, M. Iversen and D. Loxley (eds), *Literature, Politics and Theory* (London and New York: Methuen, 1986), p. 148.

20 George Orwell, 'Not counting niggers', in *The Collected Essays, Journalism and Letters of George Orwell. Volume 1. An Age Like This 1920–1940* (Harmondsworth: Penguin, 1970), p. 437.

21 David Musselwhite, 'The trial of Warren Hastings', in F. Barker, P. Hulme, M. Iversen and D. Loxley (eds), *Literature, Politics and Theory* (London and New York: Methuen, 1986), p. 77.

22 ibid, p. 83.

23 Homi K. Bhabha, 'The Other question: difference, discrimination and the discourse of colonialism', in F. Barker, P. Hulme, M. Iversen and D. Loxley, *Literature, Politics and Theory* (London and New York: Methuen, 1986), p. 156.

24 ibid, p. 151.

25 ibid, p. 153.

26 Emmanuel Lévinas, *Totality and Infinity* (Pittsburgh: Duquesne University Press, 1969).

27 Homi K. Bhabha, 'The Other question: difference, discrimination and the discourse of colonialism', in F. Barker, P. Hulme, M. Iversen and D. Loxley (eds), *Literature, Politics and Theory* (London and New York: Methuen, 1986), p. 165.

28 Homi K. Bhabha, 'Of mimicry and man: the ambivalence of colonial discourse', in James Donald and Stuart Hall (eds), *Politics and Ideology* (Milton Keynes: Open University Press, 1986), pp. 198–200.

29 Benedict Anderson, *Imagined Communities* (London: Verso, 1983).

30 See Homi K. Bhabha, 'The commitment to theory', *New Formations*, no. 5, 1988.

31 For further details on how class and gender were articulated together in an emerging national formation in the first half of the nineteenth century, and of how this combination gave rise to a particular sense of 'Englishness' and its moral economy, see Leonore Davidoff and Catherine Hall, *Family Fortunes. Men and women of the English Middle Class 1780–1850* (London: Hutchinson, 1987).

32 Catherine Hall, 'The economy of intellectual prestige: Thomas Carlyle, John Stuart Mill and the case of Governor Eyre', in *Cultural Critique*, no. 12, Spring 1989.

33 This film was part of Korda's imperialist trilogy, the other two being *Sanders of the River* (1935) and *The Drum* (1938). Imperialist adventure and exotica proved equally seductive to Hollywood: in the same decade both Gary Cooper and Errol Flynn rode out to 'man' the Indian frontier (this time in the sub-Continent rather than on the Great Plains) in such films as *The Lives of a Bengal Lancer* (1935) and *The Charge of the Light Brigade* (1936).

34 This shift was most symbolically marked in the long, drawn-out debate between John Stuart Mill and Thomas Carlyle over the

Morant Bay insurrection in Jamaica in 1865 and its suppression by Governor Eyre. Once again, as in the Hastings case, the native, Anglo-centric view publicly triumphed over the liberal, pluralist, agnostic perspective.

35 John Williams, 'White riots: the English football fan abroad', in A. Tomlinson and G. Whannel (eds), *Off The Ball* (London: Pluto, 1986), p. 17.

36 A parallel reading of Dick Hebdige's *Cut'n'Mix* (London: Comedia/Routledge, 1987) and Paul Gilroy's *There Ain't No Black in the Union Jack* (London: Hutchinson, 1987) forcibly underlines not only the necessity to rethink the nature of contemporary British culture but also the very concept of 'Englishness'.

37 Walter Benjamin, *Paris. Capital of the Nineteenth-century*. This massive, but incomplete, study of the metropolitan experience – the Italian edition is over 1,100 pages – largely consists of a collage of notes, observations, citations, jottings and short sketches. It has been published in German, *Das Passagen-Werk* (Frankfurt am Main: Suhrkamp Verlag, 1982), and Italian, *Parigi. Capitale del XIX secolo* (Turin: Einaudi, 1986).

38 Andreas Huyssen has justly pointed to these 'most interesting and yet undeveloped ideas' of Benjamin's in *After the Great Divide* (London: Macmillan, 1988, pp. 13–14 and pp. 152–6).

39 William Gaunt, *The Aesthetic Adventure* (Harmondsworth: Penguin, 1957) p. 16. The last point recalls my personal participation in mod, early '60s flâneurship when, as teenage boys, we scuffed the cuffs of new shirts with razors to give them a certain worldly 'edge'.

40 For the short season of literary modernism in British culture in the first two decades of the present century, see Michael H. Levenson, *A Genealogy of Modernism* (Cambridge: Cambridge University Press, 1986).

41 See Levenson, op. cit., pp. 123–36.

42 For a general overview of the term, see Malcolm Bradbury and James McFarlane, 'The name and nature of modernism' in Bradbury and McFarlane (eds), *Modernism* (Harmondsworth: Penguin, 1976). For a more personal account in a Marxist vein, see Marshall Berman's *All That Is Solid Melts Into Air* (London: Verso, 1983), together with Perry Anderson's polemical reply, 'Modernity and revolution' in C. Nelson and L. Grossberg (eds) *Marxism and the Interpretation of Culture* (Urbana and Chicago: University of Illinois Press, 1988; London: Macmillan, 1988).

43 See Leonore Davidoff and Catherine Hall, *Family Fortunes. Men and women of the English Middle Class 1780–1850* (London: Hutchinson, 1987), pp. 188–91.

44 John Barrell, *The Dark Side of the Landscape* (Cambridge: Cambridge University Press, 1983).

45 The concept of the 'natural and the national' comes from Simon Barker, 'Images of the sixteenth and seventeenth centuries as a history of the present', in F. Barker, P. Hulme, M. Iversen and D. Loxley (eds), *Literature, Politics and Theory* (London and New

York: Methuen, 1986) p. 175. For further, contemporary, evidence of the classical, natural, order of patrician 'Englishness', see the allegorical photographs and comments in Karen Knorr's 'The stamp of the breed', in *Ten.8*, no. 29.

46 So, in folk music theory urban song is eventually accepted into the canon as workers' or industrial songs; see A. L. Lloyd, *Folk Song in England* (London: Paladin, 1975).

47 Dick Hebdige, 'Towards a cartography of taste 1935–1962', in *Hiding in the Light* (London and New York: Comedia/Routledge, 1988).

48 For further details, see Barry Curtis, 'One continuous interwoven story (The Festival of Britain)', and Owen Gavin and Andy Lowe, 'Designing desire – planning, power and the Festival of Britain', *Block 11*, Winter 1985/6.

49 The tower is the 167-foot high mausoleum of Qabus, built in 1006 in then eastern Persia, described by Robert Bryon in *The Road to Oxiana* (1937). In the same decade Graham Greene went to West Africa (*Journey Without Maps*, 1936) and Evelyn Waugh to British Guiana, Brazil, Abyssinia and East Africa; for details see Paul Fussell, *Abroad. British Literary Travelling Between the Wars* (New York and Oxford: Oxford University Press, 1980).

50 Paul Fussell, ibid., p. 151.

51 Francis Mulhern, *The Moment of 'Scrutiny'* (London: Verso, 1979), p. 171.

52 Quoted in Raymond Williams, *Culture and Society* (Harmondsworth: Penguin, 1961), p. 247.

53 Bill Schwarz, 'Cultural studies: The case for the humanities', in J. Finch and M. Rustin, *A Degree of Choice? Higher Education and the Right to Learn* (Harmondsworth: Penguin, 1986) p. 174.

54 Perry Anderson, 'Components of the national culture', *New Left Review*, no. 50, 1968.

55 Raymond Williams, *The Long Revolution* (Harmondsworth: Penguin, 1965), p. 364.

56 See Bill Schwarz's '"The people" in history: the Communist Party Historians' Group, 1945–56', in R. Johnson, G. McLennan, B. Schwarz and D. Sutton (eds), *Making Histories. Studies in History-Writing and Politics* (London: Hutchinson, 1982).

57 See R. Samuel, 'British marxist historians 1', *New Left Review*, no. 120, 1980.

58 Bill Scharwz, '"The people" in history: the Communist Party Historians' Group, 1945–56', in R. Johnson, *et al.* (eds), *Making Histories. Studies in History-Writing and Politics* (London: Hutchinson, 1982), p. 54.

59 There were exceptions. Hobsbawm wrote a book on jazz – *The Jazz Scene* (1961), but, and perhaps this was symptomatic, under the pseudonym of Francis Newton.

60 Bill Schwarz, '"The people" in history: the Communist Party Historians' Group, 1945–56', in R. Johnson, *et al.* (eds), *Making Histories. Studies in History-Writing and Politics* (London:

Hutchinson, 1982), p. 74. This heroic and romanticized view of the past is clearly contested from other experiences of working-class life, see in particular Carolyn Steedman, *Landscape for a Good Woman. A Story of Two Lives* (London: Virago, 1986), and Terence Davies' film *Distant Voices, Still Lives* (1988); both cases significantly refer to a female eye/I.

61 See in particular Schwarz on the remarkable parallel concerns of *Scrutiny* and the British Marxist historians of the period, op. cit. pp. 61–5.

62 The momentous cultural impact of 'mechanical reproduction' on our overall sense of the modern world had, of course, been established by Walter Benjamin in 1936 in his famous essay, 'The work of art in the age of mechanical reproduction'. Many of us are still exploring the implications of what Benjamin said and suggested there.

63 The quote on our common inheritance comes from Graham Swift, *Waterland* (London: Picador, 1984), p. 16.

64 A. Gramsci, *Prison Notebooks* (London: Lawrence & Wishart, 1971). *Quaderni del Carcere* (Turin: Einaudi, 1975), pp. 2139–81.

65 The quote comes from Zygmunt Bauman's reflections on the nature and effects of historical memory in the first chapter of his *Memories of Class* (London: Routledge & Kegan Paul, 1982).

66 Gramsci's own example was that of the popularity of foreign authors in popular reading habits in Italy. He suggested that this reflected the absence of Italian intellectuals from the formation of an Italian national popular culture; they had failed to respond, to be 'organic', to such popular tastes.

67 J. B. Priestley, *English Journey* (Harmondsworth: Penguin, 1984), p. 129.

68 Walter Benjamin, 'The work of art in the age of mechanical reproduction', in *Illuminations* (London: Fontana, 1970), p. 223.

69 See Dick Hebdige, *Hiding in the Light* (London and New York: Comedia/Routledge, 1988); Iain Chambers, *Popular Culture: The Metropolitan Experience* (London and New York: Methuen, 1986); Duncan Webster, *Looka Yonder* (London and New York: Comedia/Routledge, 1988); Angela McRobbie (ed), *Zoot Suits and Second-Hand Dresses: An Anthology of Music and Fashion* (London: Macmillan, 1989).

70 E. J. Hobsbawm, *The Age of Empire: 1875–1914* (London: Weidenfeld & Nicolson, 1987). Similarly sharp in verdict is Hobsbawm's denial in the same book of the influence of avant-garde art on urban, mass culture, cf. James Joll's review 'Goodbye to all that', *The New York Review of Books*, 14 April 1988.

71 Duncan Webster, *Looka Yonder* (London and New York: Comedia/Routledge, 1988), p. 180.

72 See Gayatri Chakravorty Spivak, 'Subaltern studies: deconstructing historiography', in *In Other Worlds* (New York and London: Methuen, 1987).

73 Benedict Anderson, *Imagined Communities* (London: Verso, 1983), p. 40.

74 On the constructed and 'artificial' character of 'roots' in
    contemporary metropolitan culture, see Kobena Mercer's 'Black
    hair style/politics', *New Formations*, no. 3, 1987.
75 There are no 'cultural products, in an era when the economic has
    itself become cultural, and culture is an industry, that are not
    simultaneously items in the inventory of contemporary political
    economy': Clive Dilnot, 'Design, industry and the economy since
    1945', quoted in Kathy Myers, *Understains. The Sense and Seduction
    of Advertising* (London: Comedia, 1986), p. 149. At the heart of this
    shift lies the 'new anthropology of consumption' that characterizes
    the more flexible and dialogic sense of both modern production
    and the present day ecologies of differential consumption. This has
    recently been defined as 'post-Fordism', see Robin Murray, 'Life
    after Henry (Ford)', *Marxism Today*, October 1988; and Peter
    Wollen, 'Cinema/Americanism/the robot', in *New Formations*, no. 8,
    Summer 1989.
76 Zygmunt Bauman, *Memories of Class* (London: Routledge & Kegan
    Paul, 1982), p. 197.
77 T. F. Lindsay and Michael Harrington, *The Conservative Party,
    1918–1970* (New York: 1974), quoted in M. J. Wiener, *English
    Culture and the Decline of the Industrial Spirit, 1850–1980* (Cambridge:
    Cambridge University Press, 1981), p. 98.
78 The classic statement on the native roots of Liberal-Democratic
    theory in 'possessive individualism' and the 'market' is C. B.
    Macpherson's *The Political Theory of Possessive Individualism* (Oxford:
    Oxford University Press, 1962).
79 E. P. Thompson, *Writing by Candlelight* (London: The Merlin Press,
    1980), p. 256.

Some metropolitan tales

1 Lea Vergine,'Paesaggio con rovine' in Donatella Mazzoleni (ed.),
   La città e l'immaginario (Rome: Officina, 1985), p. 30.
2 Walter Benjamin, *Das Passagen-Werk*, in Italian *Parigi. Capitale del
   XIX secolo* (Turin: Einaudi, 1986), p. 593.
3 Simone de Beauvoir, *The Prime of Life* (Harmondsworth: Penguin,
   1966), p. 135.
4 Quoted in Christopher Butler, *After The Wake* (Oxford: Clarendon
   Press, 1980), pp. 165–6.
5 Carolyn Steedman, *Landscape for a Good Woman. A Story of Two Lives*
   (London: Virago, 1986), p. 123.
6 Roland Barthes, *Empire of Signs* (New York: Hill & Wang, 1982),
   p. 31.
7 Lidia Curti, 'Imported Utopias', in Z. Baransky and R. Lumley
   (eds), *Culture and Conflict in Postwar Italy. Essays in Popular and Mass
   Culture* (London: Macmillan, 1990).
8 This is particularly the case with traditional industrial cities. All of
   them are experiencing inner-city decay and depopulation.

Examples of attempted rejuvenation – Liverpool, Detroit and London's Docklands, for example – invariably involve attempts to be linked into the metropolitan network. This means that such urban centres are not present so much in their own right, but re-emerge in fragmented form inside the languages of contemporary architecture, art galleries and leisure cultures and a generalized urban æstheticism.

9 As Raymond Williams once suggested: 'In what is then a tension, a present experienced as tension, we use the contrast of country and city to ratify an unresolved division and conflict of impulses, which it might be better to face in its own terms.' Raymond Williams, *The Country and the City* (London: Chatto & Windus, 1973), p. 297.

10 Massimo Cacciari, *Metropolis* (Rome: Officina, 1973). See also David Frisby, *Fragments of Modernity* (Cambridge: Polity Press, 1985).

11 This might initially seem a strange proposition, particularly as I myself am so sceptical of the metaphysical and 'universalist' pretensions of critical thought. There is a paradox or double-bind here. To deconstruct the myth of the metropolis in order to dismantle the idea of a homogeneous culture ('the city is homogeneous only in appearance', Benjamin), perhaps involves an initial belief in its existence. I return to this double-bind in anti-metaphysical thought in the next chapter.

12 The expressions 'flat materialism' and time 'without memory' are Siegfried Kracauer's, in Frisby, *Fragments of Modernity* (Cambridge: Polity Press, 1985).

13 Kracauer, ibid., p. 163.

14 Simmel, ibid., p. 103.

15 Particularly in evidence in the third volume of *Capital* and in the *Grundrisse*; see Gianni Carchia, *La legittimazione dell'arte* (Naples: Guida, 1982), also Karl Marx, *Grundrisse* (Harmondsworth: Penguin, 1973), pp. 533–44.

16 Hans-Georg Gadamer, 'La dialettica platonica e la politica'. This comes from the first in a series of lectures given by the German philosopher on Plato's dialectics at the Istituto Italiano per gli Studi Filosofici in Naples in January 1989.

17 Paul Virilio and Sylvere Lotringer, *Pure War* (New York: Semiotext(e), 1983).

18 Ed Cohen, 'The "hyperreal" vs. the "really real": if European intellectuals stop making sense of American culture can we still dance?' *Cultural Studies*, vol. 3, no. 1, January 1989.

19 Maurice Blanchot, *The Writing of the Disaster* (Lincoln and London: University of Nebraska Press, 1986) p. 60.

20 Written with Lidia Curti, Stromboli, Easter 1984.

21 Paul Virilio, *L'espace critique* (Paris: Christian Bourgois, 1984).

22 Dolf Sternberger, *Panorama del XIX secolo* (Bologna: il Mulino, 1985).

23 Meaghan Morris, 'At Henry Parkes Motel', *Cultural Studies*, vol. 2, no. 1, January 1988, p. 41. The recognition of the alterity of nature, of it being irreducible to our social measure and sense, ultimately

to our interference, has given rise to a more complex dialogue with the environment than that of simple adjustment. This is frequently defined as 'deep ecology' to distinguish it from shallow, anthropocentric, versions. See, for example, Andrew Brennan, *Thinking About Nature: An Investigation of Nature, Value and Ecology* (London: Routledge, 1988).

24 See the concluding chapter, 'Metaphysics and the Philosophy of Science', in Roy Bhaskar's *A Realist Theory of Science* (Leeds: Leeds Books, 1975).

25 For a stimulating overview of this question see the chapter 'The Demise of Experience: Fiction as Stranger than Truth', in Alice A. Jardine, *Gynesis* (Ithaca and London: Cornell University Press, 1985).

26 *Aurora*, aphorism 44.

27 Such a reading of the 'eternal return' owes much to Pierre Klossowski's commentary on Nietzsche elaborated in the 1950s. Subsequently collected in *Un si funeste désir* (Paris: Gallimard, 1963) and *Nietzsche et le cercle vicieux* (Paris: Mercure de France, 1969), this work extensively developed the concept of the simulacrum which later influenced a whole generation of French intellectuals, including Foucault, Deleuze and Blanchot. I have taken these details from Furio Di Paola's important afterword, 'Noialtri Barocchi e Baudrillard', in Jean Baudrillard, *Simulacri e Impostura* (Bologna: Cappelli, 1980). I return to a discussion of Nietzsche and the ontological 'truth' of appearances in the next chapter.

28 Benjamin, *Parigi. Capitale del XIX secolo* (Turin: Einaudi, 1986).

29 See G. A. Cohen, *Karl Marx's Theory of History* (Oxford: Clarendon Press, 1978), pp. 96–8.

30 Karl Marx, *Grundrisse* (Harmondsworth: Penguin, 1973), p. 162. Or, as he puts it in the first volume of *Capital*:

> Man opposes himself to Nature as one of her own forces, setting in motion arms and legs, head and hands, the natural forces of his body, in order to appropriate Nature's productions in a form adapted to his own wants. By thus acting on the external world and changing it, he at the same time changes his own nature. (London: Lawrence & Wishart, 1970, p. 173).

For further discussion on the profoundly social production, mediation and construction of 'nature' in Marx, see Alfred Schmidt's *The Concept of Nature in Marx* (London: New Left Books, 1971).

31 Gianni Vattimo, *La fine della modernità* (Milan: Garzanti, 1985), p. 31.

32 This has been particularly in evidence in popular music and in the perpetual debate it has had with itself over musical 'authenticity' and the threat of technology. It can be found in every moment of its history, from crooning to punk. See Simon Frith, 'Art versus technology: the strange case of popular music', in *Media, Culture and Society*, vol. 8, no. 3, July 1986.

33 Kathy Myers, *Understains. The Sense and Seduction of Advertising*, (London: Comedia, 1986), p. 5.

34 Karl Marx, *Grundrisse* (Harmondsworth: Penguin, 1973), p. 540.

35 ibid., pp. 541–2.

36 Gregor McLennan, *Marxism and the Methodologies of History* (London: Verso, 1981), p. 166. A comment by Nietzsche is worth citing here: 'We Germans are hegelians even if Hegel had never existed to the degree that, unlike the Latins, we instinctively attribute to the future, to progress, a deeper meaning, a richer value than there is' (*The Gay Science*).

37 This, of course, raises the question, debated in the 1970s by Lucio Colletti, for example, whether the 'logic' of contradiction is an acceptable historical category, that is, whether there is a 'dialectic' to history. Further, are contradictions the essential links that explain the chains of capitalism or are they present everywhere in social development? If we opt for the second proposal then quite clearly contradictions will not end with capitalism, there will be no final reconciliation.

38 Alessandro Dal Lago, 'The demise of the Revolutionary Imaginary?', in *Differentia*, no. 1, Autumn 1986, pp. 49–50.

39 Karl Marx, *Grundrisse* (Harmondsworth: Penguin, 1973), p. 162.

40 Maurizio Ferraris, *Tracce Nichilismo Moderno Postmoderno* (Milan: Multhipla Edizioni, 1983), p. 60. The anti-metaphysical drive, if not relentlessly driven home, is nevertheless clearly evident in Marx's mature writings. It is not always so clear whether the same can be said of much subsequent Marxist analyses and politics.

41 Michel Foucault, 'Nietzsche, genealogy, history', in *Language, Counter-Memory, Practice: Selected Essays and Interviews* (Ithaca: Cornell University Press, 1977), p. 148; translation modified.

42 Georg Simmel, *La moda* (Rome: Riuniti, 1985).

43 To which we can add Walter Benjamin's observation: 'Every fashion couples the living body with the inorganic world. In dealing with the living fashion imposes the rights of the corpse. Fetishism, which rests on the *sex-appeal* of the inorganic, is its vital nerve.' Walter Benjamin, *Parigi. Capitale del XIX secolo* (Turin: Einaudi, 1986), p. 124.

44 For an excellent account of the history of fashion and its social and æsthetic possibilities in the modern world, see Elizabeth Wilson, *Adorned in Dreams* (London: Virago, 1985).

45 The emphasis is on the popular here because, of course, there exists a whole male tradition of aristocratic and bohemian dandies, *flâneurs* and æsthetes whose sartorial inspiration runs from Beau Brummel to Giorgio Armani.

46 From a talk at Bristol's Watershed on the occasion of *The Face* exhibition in the autumn of 1985.

47 With this I also intend a self-criticism towards the over-emphasis on male subcultures and the under-emphasis on the more extensive dimensions of gender and sexuality in my own examination of the cultural economy of pop music in *Urban*

Rhythms: Pop Music and Popular Culture (London: Macmillan, 1985; New York: St Martin's Press, 1986).

48 Janice Winship, *Inside Women's Magazines* (London and New York: Pandora, 1987) p. 149.

49 What this might mean in terms of contemporary representations and images can be gauged, for example, from the often very different ethnic, gendered, sexual, class and national experiences exposed on the pages of the photographic magazine *Ten.8*.

50 See Janice Winship, *Inside Women's Magazines* (London and New York: Pandora, 1987), pp. 152–4.

51 This, in turn, is another, possible reply to Hebdige's passionate and noble defence of 'Planet One' against the dead simulation of life on the postmodern world of 'Planet Two'. Perhaps the metaphor is itself a trap. Perhaps the *topos* is not divided by light-years of travel between two worlds, but simultaneously shared, even experienced by the same bodies, the same subjects. To employ another science fiction motif, perhaps we concurrently inhabit 'parallel universes' to which there are no obvious 'entry' and 'exit' signs. In a perpetual (semi-) osmosis we are caught up in complex transformations of sense across the membranes of these universes in which *The Face* is only a tiny part of the allegory. Like the skull of the dead in Walter Benjamin's study of baroque theatre, it has no symbolic freedom of expression; it signifies the enigma of a history in which both it and we are caught, and in which we have no choice but to struggle to make our own.

52 For a further discussion of marginality, ethnicity and the question of representative imagery, see Isaac Julien and Kobena Mercer, 'Introduction – De Margin and De Centre', *Screen*, vol. 29, no. 4, Autumn 1988.

53 For difference may turn out to involve only a temporary split in an eventual singularity. Certain writings – those of Nietzsche, Barthes, Lacan, Derrida and Foucault, for example – rarely permit female specificity to put in question the male articulation, organisation, paradigm, unity and ultimate indifference to women; see Naomi Schor, 'Dreaming dissymmetry: Barthes, Foucault, and Sexual difference', in Alice Jardine and Paul Smith (eds), *Men in Feminism* (London and New York: Methuen, 1987).

54 The reference here is to Richard Hamilton's Pop Art pictorial parable of domestic consumption, *$he* (1958–61).

55 Judith Williamson, *Decoding Advertisements* (London and Boston: Marion Boyars, 1978).

56 Here, from the future, is a woman's recollection of advertising (now banned):

> What was in them was promise. They dealt in transformations; they suggested an endless series of possibilities, extending like reflections in two mirrors set facing one another, stretching on, replica after replica, to the vanishing point. They suggested one adventure after another, one improvement after another, one man after another. They suggested rejuvenation, pain overcome

and transcended, endless love. The real promise in them was immortality.

Margaret Atwood, *The Handmaid's Tale* (London: Virago, 1987), p. 165.

57 See Rosemary Kowalski, 'Madonna: woman is the message', in *OneTwoThreeFour*, no. 3, Autumn 1986, p. 63; and Patrizia Calefato, 'Fashion, the passage, the body', *Cultural Studies*, vol. 2, no. 2, May 1988.

58 Luce Irigaray, *The Sex Which Is Not One* (Ithaca: Cornell University Press, 1985), p. 76. This recalls and extends Joan Riviere's 1929 article 'Woman as a masquerade', reprinted in Victor Burgin, James Donald and Cora Kaplan (eds), *Formations of Fantasy* (London: Methuen, 1986). For the connection between woman as masquerade, as mask, and her position as the enigma and unknowable 'other' in modern critical thought, see Stephen Heath 'Joan Riviere and the masquerade', ibid., and Chapter 5 in this book.

59 Mary Russo, 'Female Grotesques: Carnival and Theory', in Teresa de Lauretis (ed.) *Feminist Studies/Critical Studies* (Bloomington: Indiana University Press, 1986), p. 224. ·

60 The term 'white negro' was coined by the American writer Norman Mailer in *Advertisements for Myself* (London: Panther, 1968). The quotes on 'cool' and 'economic raids' come from Ned Polsky, *Hustlers, Beats and Others* (Harmondsworth: Penguin, 1971), pp. 151 and 149 respectively.

61 The diverse contributions to the history of 'black modernism' – from be-bop and R&B to contemporary dub, scratch music and black videos such as Sankofa's *Territories* (1985) – can be read as an extensive and largely autonomous discourse on the languages, images and representative possibilities of contemporary, urban, culture. Here a particular ethnic marginality has often become the unacknowledged source and centre of a metropolitan æsthetic. On 'ragamuffin' culture, see Kwesi Owusu, 'Ragamuffin', *Marxism Today*, September 1989.

62 Add to this the metropolitan club mixes of jazz, house, rap, raregroove and scratch, the black postmodern mélange of Soul II Soul, or the retro-soul style and '50s imagery of a black British group like The Pasedenas, and you have some idea of the heterogeneous possibilities thrown up through the use of sonorial and cultural memories and traditions within black music and British pop.

63 See D. Pathi, 'Punjabi Goes Pop', *The Face*, March 1986; S. Steward and S. Garratt, *Signed, Sealed and Delivered: True Life Stories of Women in Pop* (London: Pluto, 1984); D. Hebdige, *Cut'n'Mix* (London and New York: Comedia/Methuen, 1987); I. Chambers, 'British pop: some tracks from the other side of the record', in J. Lull (ed.), *Popular Music and Communication* (London and Beverly Hills: Sage, 1987). The definition of Bangra music comes from David Toop, *Chasing Rainbows – A Nation and Its Music* (London:

Comedia, 1986), p. 6.
64 Jazzie B interviewed in Lindsay Baker's 'Funk like a Dred', *The Face*, April 1989, p. 64.
65 Marilyn Frye, *The Politics of Reality* (New York: The Crossing Press, 1984), quoted in Jane Gaines, 'White privileges and looking relations: race and gender in feminist film theory', *Screen*, vol. 29, no. 4, Autumn 1988, p. 13.
66 Jane Gaines, ibid.
67 Walter Benjamin, 'Theses on the philosophy of history', in *Illuminations* (London: Fontana, 1970), p. 259.
68 Gianni Vattimo, 'Ma non verrà l'apocalisse da mass media', *La Stampa. Universo Informatica*, maggio 1988, p. 6.
69 Hans Magnus Enzensberger, 'Constituents of a theory of the media', *New Left Review*, no. 64, 1970.
70 The most noted exponents of the 'third wave', that is of the inevitable resolution of existing social contradictions through 'soft' (i.e. information) technology, are Alvin Toffler and André Gorz. For an extensive overview of the whole discussion, see Boris Frankel, *The Post-Industrial Utopians* (Cambridge: Polity Press, 1987).
71 Gianni Vattimo, *La fine della modernità* (Milan: Garzanti, 1985), p. 17; translated as *The End of Modernity* (Oxford: Polity Press, 1988).
72 Paolo Virno at the conference *1990: fuga dalla città? Metropoli diffusa o nuovi localismi?*, Rome, 21 April 1989.
73 Alice A. Jardine, *Gynesis* (New York: Cornell University Press, 1985), p. 25. 'Gynesis' is the neologism that Jardine uses to indicate 'the putting into discourse of "woman"'.
74 See Elizabeth Grosz, 'The "people of the book": representation and alterity in Emmanuel Lévinas', *Art and Text*, 26, September–November 1987.

A handful of sand

1 Michel Foucault, *Microfisica del potere* (Turin: Einaudi, 1977), p. 28.
2 Robert M. Pirsig, *Zen and the Art of Motorcycle Maintenance* (New York: Bantam, 1981), p. 61. For a discussion of this book in the context of postmodernism and Nietzschean thought, see Christopher Norris, *Deconstruction. Theory & Practice* (London and New York: Methuen, 1982), pp. 61–4.
3 Walter Benjamin, *Parigi. Capitale del XIX secolo* (Turin: Einaudi, 1986), p. 591.
4 Friedrich Nietzsche, from *The Gay Science*, in *A Nietzsche Reader* (Harmondsworth: Penguin, 1977), pp. 209–10.
5 Giovanna Borradori, '"Weak thought" and the "Aesthetics of quotationism": the Italian shift from deconstruction', *Working Paper* No. 6, Fall 1986, Center for Twentieth Century Studies.

6 Edmund Burke, 'Preface' to the second edition of *A Philosophical Enquiry into the Origin of Our Ideas of the Sublime and Beautiful* (facsimile edition of the second edition of 1759; New York: Garland, 1971), p. vi.

7 Friedrich Nietzsche, *Beyond Good and Evil* (Harmondsworth: Penguin, 1973), p. 52.

8 Gianni Carchia, *La legittimazione dell'arte* (Naples: Guida, 1982), p. 63.

9 Sergio Givone, *Storia dell'estetica* (Bari: Laterza, 1988) p. 38. For further discussion on the sublime in an explicitly postmodern context, see the contributions by Jean-François Lyotard and Philippe Lacoue-Labarthe in *ICA Documents 4. Postmodernism* (London: Institute of Contemporary Arts, 1986).

10 'Let us remember that the significance of Kantian subjectivism as a whole lies in its objective intention, its attempt to salvage objectivity by means of an analysis of subjective moments.' Theodor Adorno, *Aesthetic Theory* (London: Routledge & Kegan Paul, 1986), p. 14.

11 Friedrich Nietzsche, *Twilight of the Idols*, in *A Nietzsche Reader* (Harmondsworth: Penguin, 1977), p. 145.

12 Edmund Burke, *A Philosophical Enquiry into the Origin of Our Ideas of the Sublime and Beautiful* (facsimile edition of the second edition of 1759; New York: Garland, 1971), p. 58.

13 However, Heidegger would probably not have been too happy with this association. He sought to establish a shared objective in Kantian and Nietzschean æsthetics, and considered Nietzsche's attack against Kant's 'disinterested' concept of the beautiful to be based on a misinterpretation inherited from Schopenhauer; see chapter 15 of Martin Heidegger, *Nietzsche*, vol. 1 (London: Routledge & Kegan Paul, 1981). I personally think that here, as elsewhere in his dealings with Nietzsche, Heidegger is seeking to tame the potential of a possible confrontation; see note 65.

14 For an interpretation of postmodernism as a celebration of commodified kitsch, see Frederic Jameson's neo-Lukácsian analysis in 'Postmodernism or the cultural logic of late capitalism', *New Left Review*, no. 145, 1984.

15 This, for example, is the criticism advanced by Dick Hebdige in his analysis of the London style magazine *The Face* in 'The bottom line on Planet One', *Ten.8*, no. 19, 1985, now republished in *Hiding in the Light* (London and New York: Comedia/Routledge, 1988).

16 Allan Megill, *Prophets of Extremity. Nietzsche, Heidegger, Foucault, Derrida* (Berkeley, Los Angeles and London: University of California Press, 1985), p. 10.

17 ibid, p. 10.

18 It should be noted that Megill's use of the term 'æstheticism' is quite distinct from the way Dick Hebdige uses it in his essay on the sublime: 'The impossible object. Towards a sociology of the sublime', *New Formations*, no. 1, Spring 1987. In fact, by characterizing as 'æstheticism' the Nietzschean proposition that the

world is a work of (our) art (subsequently extended in their
different ways by Heidegger, Foucault and Derrida), it has almost
the opposite meaning from its place in Hebdige's argument where
'æstheticism' stands rather for the local and distinct experiments in
language, form and style that characterize the metropolitan,
European avant-garde of the nineteenth and twentieth centuries;
see Hebdige op. cit., p. 52. In other words, while in the
Nietzschean inheritance art dissolves into the world, opening on to
the idea that the world is constituted by language, or discourse or
texts, in the more restricted situation indicated in Hebdige's use of
the term it is precisely because the world initially provides a non-
æsthetic framing or background that avant-garde and modernist art
is able to stand out and become the object of æsthetic attention.
Around this distinction can readily be identified the sweep of the
two currents that flow into the critical storm over 'modernism' and
'postmodernism'.

19 Allan Megill, *Prophets of Extremity. Nietzsche, Heidegger, Foucault, Derrida* (Berkeley, Los Angeles and London: University of California Press, 1985), p. 4.
20 ibid, p. 33.
21 Edmond Jabès, *Le petit livre de la subversion hors de soupçon* (Paris: Editions Gallimard, 1982).
22 On contemporary travel and *travail* (labour, hardship, suffering), see Meaghan Morris, 'At Henry Parkes Motel', *Cultural Studies*, vol. 2, no. 1, January 1988; and Lawrence Grossberg, 'Wandering audiences, nomadic critics', *Cultural Studies*, vol. 2, no. 3, October 1988.
23 Paul Virilio, *L'horizon négatif. Essai du dromoscopie* (Paris: Editions Galilée, 1984).
24 Jean Baudrillard, *Amérique* (Paris: Editions Grasset, 1986); *America* (London: Verso, 1988). I am translating here from the Italian edition: *L'America* (Milan: Feltrinelli, 1987), p. 70.
25 Roberto Calasso, 'Monologo fatale', postscript to F. Nietzsche, *Ecce Homo* (Milan: Adelphi, 1969), p. 175.
26 Henri Lefebvre, *Le manifeste différentialiste* (Paris: Editions Gallimard, 1970). Again, I am translating from the Italian edition: *Il manifesto differenzialista* (Bari: Dedalo, 1980), p. 49.
27 Karl Marx, *Grundrisse* (Harmondsworth: Penguin, 1973), pp. 100–2.
28 Henri Lefebvre, *La fin de l'histoire* (Paris: Les Éditions de Minuit, 1970). The Italian edition that I am using is: *La Fine della Storia* (Milan: Sugar, 1972), pp. 94–5.
29 Friedrich Nietzsche, *Ecce Homo* (Harmondsworth: Penguin, 1979), p. 112 .
30 Friedrich Nietzsche, from *Human, All Too Human*, in *A Nietzsche Reader* (Harmondsworth: Penguin, 1977), p. 55.
31 Franco Rella, 'La ragione e il potere', in *Sapere e Potere*, vol. 2 (Milan: multhipla edizioni, 1984) p. 88. On a personal note, it is this dimension in Afro-American and Afro-Caribbean music that I sought to point to some years ago in my book, *Urban Rhythms: Pop*

Music and Popular Culture (London: Macmillan, 1985; New York: St Martin's Press, 1986); not to propose it as a mind-less *body* music, as some have suggested, but to underline a different cultural sense of the body and consciousness: one generally repressed and robbed of recognition in the hegemonic discourses of white European, and European-derived, societies.

32 ibid, p. 89.

33 Roberto Calasso 'Monologo fatale', postscript to F. Nietzsche, *Ecce Homo* (Milan: Adelphi, 1969), p. 200.

34 Friedrich Nietzsche, *Human, All Too Human*, in *A Nietzsche Reader* (Harmondsworth: Penguin, 1977), pp. 29–30.

35 According to Heidegger, it was Hegel's merit to push the relationship between *logos*, as a teleological instance ('onteological'), and being to its limits. To renounce metaphysics it is perhaps necessary to renounce the link between being and *logos*, and therefore the very idea of ontology, and recognize instead a relationship between finite being and temporality; what Heidegger chose to call 'ontochronology'; Paolo Virno, 'Fine dell'infinito. Il tempo tra Heidegger e Hegel', *il Manifesto*, 8 September 1988.

36 The quote comes from *Thus Spoke Zarathustra* (Harmondsworth: Penguin, 1969), p. 332.

37 Herman Melville, *Moby Dick* (Harmondsworth: Penguin, 1986), p. 262.

38 Henri Lefebvre, *Le manifeste différentialiste* (Paris: Editions Gallimard, 1970); *Il manifesto differenzialista* (Bari: Dedalo, 1980), pp. 84–5.

39 Roberto Calasso, 'Monologo Fatale', postscript to F. Nietzsche, *Ecce Homo* (Milan: Adelphi, 1969), p. 173.

40 Friedrich Nietzsche, *Beyond Good and Evil* (Harmondsworth: Penguin, 1973), p. 17.

41 This paragraph is a reworked extract from Iain Chambers, 'Rolling away from the centre towards X. Some notes on Italian philosophy, "weak thought" and postmodernism', in Z. Baransky and R. Lumley (eds), *Culture and Conflict in Postwar Italy. Essays in Popular and Mass Culture* (London: Macmillan, 1990).

42 Gianni Vattimo, 'Dialettica, differenza, pensiero debole', in G. Vattimo and P. A. Rovatti (eds), *Il pensiero debole* (Milan: Feltrinelli, 1983), p. 18.

43 Gianni Vattimo, *La fine della modernità* (Milan: Garzanti, 1985), p. 29. The English edition is: *The End of Modernity* (Oxford: Polity Press, 1988).

44 Gianni Vattimo, 'Postmodernità e fine della storia', in G. Mari (ed.), *Moderno postmoderno* (Milan: Feltrinelli, 1987), p. 99. What follows is largely an extended commentary on this important essay.

45 ibid, p. 100.

46 ibid, pp. 100–1.

47 ibid, p. 101.

48 In fact, Maurizio Ferraris observes that the debate between

modernism and postmodernism is a further form of the problematical relationship indicated by Heidegger between the *Überwindung* (overcoming, passing beyond) and *Verwindung* (overcoming, but also reimmersing, consigning yourself) of/to metaphysics. See Maurizio Ferraris, *Tracce Nichilismo Moderno Postmoderno* (Milan: multhipla edizioni, 1983), pp. 9–10.

49 Gianni Vattimo, 'Postmodernità e fine della storia', in G. Mari (ed.), *Moderno postmoderno* (Milan: Feltrinelli, 1987), p. 102.

50 ibid, p. 103.

51 Again, this, and the previous three paragraphs, is a reworked extract from Iain Chambers, 'Rolling away from the centre towards X. Some notes on Italian philosophy, "weak thought" and postmodernism', in Z. Baransky and R. Lumley (eds), *Culture and Conflict in Postwar Italy. Essays in Popular and Mass Culture* (London: Macmillan, 1990).

52 Friedrich Nietzsche, *Ecce Homo* (Harmondsworth: Penguin, 1979), p. 127.

53 Friedrich Nietzsche, *Thus Spoke Zarathustra* (Harmondsworth: Penguin, 1969), p. 89.

54 Friedrich Nietzsche, *Daybreak*, in *A Nietzsche Reader* (Harmondsworth: Penguin, 1977), p. 205.

55 Talking Heads, 'City of Dreams', *True Stories* (EMI, 1986).

56 Heidegger pointed out that the only authentic image of the truth of being that we have at our disposal is the ineluctable and constitutive instance of our death. To which we can add Max Horkheimer's observation that death 'demonstrates the powerlessness of all meaning-giving metaphysics and any theodicy': quoted in Alfred Schmidt, *The Concept of Nature in Marx* (London: New Left Books, 1971), p. 36.

57 This point has been well established by Megill in *Prophets of Extremity. Nietzsche, Heidegger, Foucault, Derrida* (Berkeley, Los Angeles and London: University of California Press, 1985). Franco Rella also makes the same point against both Habermas (naturally enough) and (more significantly) Vattimo's philosophy of 'weak thought' and its 'ontology of decline'; Franco Rella, *Limina. Il pensiero e le cose* (Milan: Feltrinelli, 1987), p. 23.

58 Allan Megill, *Prophets of Extremity. Nietzsche, Heidegger, Foucault, Derrida* (Berkeley, Los Angeles and London: University of California Press, 1985), p. 296. Note, Megill says this of Nietzsche, but I think it is legitimate to extend the argument to Marx and much Marxist thought.

59 At this point, it is customary to refer to the subsequent crisis of positivism in the natural and social sciences in the late-nineteenth and early twentieth centuries when earlier certainties were eroded by the advent of evolutionism, relativity, psychoanalysis, and, although this tends to be mentioned less frequently, mass democracy and mass warfare.

60 Martin Heidegger, 'The Question Concerning Technology', in Martin Heidegger, *The Question Concerning Technology and Other*

Essays (New York: Harper & Row, 1977), p. 14.
61 ibid, p. 16.
62 'Woodpaths' (*Holzwege*) was the title of a collection of essays published by Heidegger in 1950.
63 Emmanuel Lévinas, *Totality and Infinity* (Pittsburgh: Duquesne University Press, 1969), p. 47.
64 This is not the version that Vattimo gives. Although I am full of admiration for Vattimo's reading of Heidegger, of opening up his language and perspectives towards a less nostalgic relationship with present realities, I feel that Heidegger's own insistence on the problem of authentic 'being' is less generous in its contemporary concerns than Vattimo gives it credit for.
65 In discussing the concept of *die Gerechtigkeit* ('justness, rightness, equity'), Gillian Rose observes that 'Zarathustra's discourse is the jurisprudence of this law beyond the opposition of rational versus revealed', and in this light she goes on to criticize the Heideggerean concept of the 'event' of being:

> Heidegger . . . treats Nietzsche's strategy as if it were dispensable, and this summary treatment of Nietzsche's drama is deeply allied to Heidegger's repeated denial that Nietzsche's ultimate concern is with *die Gerechtigkeit*. He does not take Nietzsche's thought 'forward' by 'stepping back' and renewing its erstwhile beginning: he ruins it – by turning the history of the relation between law and morality into the singular event, *das Ereignis*

Gillian Rose, *Dialectic of Nihilism, Post-Structuralism and Law* (Oxford: Blackwell, 1984), pp. 90–1. This criticism of the reductive (and conservative) disposition of Heidegger's thinking, where the diverse and extraneous is reduced to a homogeneous discourse – that refuses and defuses, for example in Heidegger's two volumes on Nietzsche, the infectious connotations of the 'will to power' and the 'eternal return', as well as his predecessor's desire to be regarded as a nomad on the road towards an endless, unmarked desert, and instead attempts to pin him down as the last of the metaphysicians – is also the point consistently made by Lévinas in *Totality and Infinity*.
66 The dramatic oscillation between the limits of representation and the infinite universe of the 'will to power' was of course most tragically played out by Nietzsche himself between the completion of *Ecce Homo* in October 1888 and the moment some months later when he goes beyond himself (*Übermensch*): 'Nietzsche collapsed in the Piazza Carlo Alberti, Turin (3 January): when he recovers consciousness he is no longer sane. He sends brief letters to friends, acquaintances and public figures announcing his arrival as "Dionysos" or "the Crucified"', R. J. Hollingdale, 'Chronology of Nietzsche's Life' in F. Nietzsche, *Ecce Homo* (Harmondsworth: Penguin, 1979), p. 28.

Voices, traces, horizons

1 Michèle Le Doeuff, 'Women and philosophy', *Radical Philosophy*, no. 17, p. 11.
2 Sigmund Freud, *Totem and Taboo* (London: Routledge & Kegan Paul, 1960), p. 95.
3 Michel de Certeau, *Heterologies. Discourse on the Other* (Manchester: Manchester University Press, 1986), p. 3.
4 Quoted in Franco Rella, *Il silenzio e le parole* (Milan: Feltrinelli, 1981), p. 102.
5 Here I am paraphrasing Terry Eagleton, *Marxism and Literary Criticism* (London: New Left Books, 1976), pp. 34–5.
6 Franco Rella, *Il mito dell'altro* (Milan: Feltrinelli, 1978), p. 27.
7 The quote is from Freud's 'The uncanny', originally published in 1919, in vol. 17 of *The Standard Edition* (London: The Hogarth Press, 1925).
8 Edmond Jabès, *Un étranger avec, sous le bras, un livre de petit format*, (Paris: Gallimard, 1989); Emmanuel Lévinas, *Totality and Infinity* (Pittsburgh: Duquesne University Press, 1969).
9 Quoted in Meaghan Morris, *The Pirate's Fiancée* (London: Verso, 1988), p. 75.
10 Meaghan Morris, ibid, p. 86.
11 Otto Weininger, *Geschlecht und Charakter* ('Sex and Character'), quoted in Franco Rella, *Il silenzio e le parole* (Milan: Feltrinelli, 1981) p. 11. The use of the figure of 'woman' and 'Jew' as disruptive symbols of difference, and their place within the crisis of modernity (both in the sense of modernity experiencing a specific crisis and modernity as the epoch of crisis), has been brilliantly explored, in the context of the early twentieth-century Viennese culture of Wittgenstein, Hofmannsthal and Musil, in Franco Rella's reading of Otto Weininger's misogynist and antisemitic text published in 1903; see Rella, ibid. Andreas Huyssen has also investigated how in diverse currents of modernism 'authentic' culture has regularly been compared to the negative, feminine attributes of mass, popular culture. Here, once again, the fear of the 'masses' is the fear of nature out of control, a fear of the 'other', of the libidinous id, that achieves its sharpest metaphor in the mysterious figure of 'woman' and her sexuality, her 'nature': the threat of the unconscious and unrepresented side of society and culture to the self-identity of man, to rational discourse and intellectual order; see Andreas Huyssen 'Mass culture as women: modernism's other', in *After the Great Divide* (London: Macmillan, 1988). On 'woman' as the unknown, the unsayable, the indecipherable, as that excess which signifies the 'other' for the philosophers of crisis and difference (from Nietzsche to Derrida), and this time articulated by a woman, see Alice Jardine's *Gynesis* (New York: Cornell University Press, 1985).
12 The expression 'fusion of horizons' comes from Hans-Georg Gadamer's *Truth and Method* (London: Sheed & Ward, 1975).

13 Jonathan Rutherford, 'Who's that man', in R. Chapman and J. Rutherford (eds), *Male Order. Unwrapping Masculinity* (London; Lawrence & Wishart, 1988), p. 43.

14 Gianni Carchia, *La legittimazione dell'arte* (Naples: Guida, 1982), p. 17.

15 Emmanuel Lévinas, *Totality and Infinity* (Pittsburgh: Duquesne University Press, 1969), p. 25; translation modified.

16 See Chapter 6, 'Historicizing the postmodern: the problematizing of history', in Linda Hutcheon's *A Poetics of Postmodernism* (London and New York: Routledge, 1988).

17 Sheila Rowbotham, *Hidden from History. 300 Years of Women's Oppression and the Fight Against It* (London: Pluto, 1974).

18 Angela Carter, *The Passion of New Eve* (London: Virago, 1982), p. 53.

19 Linda Hutcheon, *A Poetics of Postmodernism* (London and New York: Routledge, 1988), p. 223.

20 Walter Benjamin in Franco Rella, *Il silenzio e le parole* (Milan: Feltrinelli, 1981), p. 146. Of course, this constructed and contingent sense of 'authenticity' is quite distinct from the common-sensical one rooted in the uninterrupted unfolding of linear time and traditions.

21 Walter Benjamin, 'Theses on the philosophy of history', in *Illuminations* (London: Fontana, 1973), p. 266

22 Hans-Georg Gadamer, 'La responsabilità al singolare', *aut aut*, 226–7, luglio–ottobre 1988, p. 42.

23 Paolo Virno at the conference *1990: fuga dalla città? Metropoli diffusa o nuovi localismi?*, Rome, 21 April 1989.

24 Friedrich Nietzsche, *Thus Spoke Zarathustra* (Harmondsworth: Penguin, 1969), p. 62.

25 'Infanzia berlinese intorno al millenovecento', in Walter Benjamin, *Immagini di città* (Turin: Einaudi, 1980) p. 76.

26 These two sentences represent a mix of Walter Benjamin, *Parigi. Capitale del XIX secolo* (Turin: Einaudi, 1986), Robert Warshow, *The Immediate Experience* (New York: Doubleday, 1962), and Franco Rella, *Metamorfosi. Immagini del pensiero* (Milan: Feltrinelli, 1984).

27 'The work of art in the age of mechanical reproduction', in W. Benjamin, *Illuminations* (London: Fontana, 1973).

28 Franco Rella, *Metamorfosi. Immagini del pensiero* (Milan: Feltrinelli,1984), p. 31.

29 Hannah Arendt, *The Human Condition* (Chicago and London: University of Chicago Press, 1958); see pp. 173–81.

30 Adriana Caverero, 'Nati per incominciare', *il Manifesto*, 13 April 1989. In the state of *atopia* we might also at this point read the conditions of being both a woman and Jewish.

31 Walter Benjamin, 'Theses on the philosophy of history', in *Illuminations*, p. 259. The English title of the Wenders film, released in 1987, was 'The Sky over Berlin'.

32 Paul Ricœur, *Time and Narrative*, vol. 3, (London: University of Chicago Press, 1988).

33 Gino Scatasta, 'Estraneo ai suoi simili', *L'Indice*, no. 5, May 1989.
    Bruce Chatwin died in 1989. He published five novels: *In Patagonia*;
    On the Black Hill; *The Viceroy of Ouidah*; *The Songlines*; *Utz*.
34 Michel de Certeau, *Heterologies. Discourse on the Other* (Manchester:
    Manchester University Press, 1986), p. 226
35 See A. J. Ayer, *Ludwig Wittgenstein* (Harmondsworth: Penguin,
    1986), p. 31.
36 Dana Polan, 'Brief encounters. Mass culture and the evacuation of
    sense' in Tania Modleski (ed.), *Studies in Entertainment. Critical
    Approaches to Mass Culture* (Bloomington and Indianapolis: Indiana
    University Press, 1986).
37 The expression 'radical linguistics of thought' comes from Franz
    Rosenzweig, *Der Stern der Erlösung* (The Star of Redemption),
    quoted in Carchia, *La legittimazione dell'arte* (Naples: Guida, 1982),
    p. 17. While the idea of the question being conserved as a question
    comes from Jacques Derrida's essay on Lévinas in *Writing and
    Difference* (Chicago: Chicago University Press, 1978).

At the centre of Fedora, a metropolis of grey stone, there is a metal building with a glass sphere in each of its rooms. Looking into each sphere one sees a blue city that is the model of another Fedora. They represent the form the city might have taken if, for one reason or another, it had not become the object we see today. In every epoch, someone seeing Fedora as it was, had imagined transforming it into an ideal city, but while he constructed his model in miniature Fedora had already changed, and what until yesterday had been a possible future was now only a toy in a glass sphere.

Italo Calvino, *Le città invisibili*

Index